Praise for *The Talented Manager*

"Adrian Furnham is one of the most prolific academics in the world, but his most exceptional talent is his ability to do research that appeals not just to academics but also to business and laypeople alike. In this collection of essays, Furnham covers an impressive list of hot management topics in an authoritative yet engaging way. Indeed, the author injects humor and science into a world so often dominated by clichés and pop psychology. There is probably no other management scientist so well equipped with facts, research evidence, and many years of business experience at the top of the game. Generations of consultants and managers will appreciate this masterpiece." – **Tomas Chamorro-Premuzic**, *New York University, USA*

"Furnham can be relied upon to come out fighting. Fists fly as misconceptions are laid to rest whilst new ideas are fertilized with insight and realism. A book about talent by a talent." – **Professor Christopher Jackson**, *University of New South Wales, Australia*

"Adrian's book is refreshing in a number of ways. It is easy reading, light-hearted, and enjoyable. Yet more than that, he starts to question some of the fundamental truths that we persist with yet know don't work. He raises good, valid objections from both a philosophical and practical perspective which if considered could lead to better outcomes, less wasted time on fools' errands and financial savings." – **Mike Haffendon**, *CEO, Strategic Dimensions, UK*

"Talent: what it is, how to find it, how to develop it, how to lead it, how to manage it, how to retain it. These are all questions that resound with anyone involved in Human Resources, Learning and Development or managing organizations. These questions, in his inimitable, accessible and witty style, have all been addressed by Professor Adrian Furnham in his new book *The Talented Manager*. All the hallmarks of another Furnham classic are here... Bite-sized morsels of pithy, relevant, funny, illuminating and engaging content, wrapped up in a package that will suit academics and business people alike." **Dr Mark Batey**, *Manchester Business School, UK*

*Also by Adrian Furnham*

*Management and Myths*
*Managing People in a Downturn*
*Learning at Work*
*Management Mumbo-Jumbo*
*Head and Heart Management*
*People Management in Turbulent Times*
*Management Intelligence*
*The Elephant in the Boardroom*
*Body Language in Business* (with Evgeniya Petrova)
*The Dark Side of Behaviour at Work* (with John Taylor)
*Leadership: All You Need To Know* (with David Pendleton)
*Bad Apples* (with John Taylor)
*The People Business*

# THE TALENTED MANAGER

*67 Gems of Business Wisdom*

**Adrian Furnham**

First published 2012 by
PALGRAVE MACMILLAN

Palgrave Macmillan in the UK is an imprint of Macmillan Publishers Limited, registered in England, company number 785998, of Houndmills, Basingstoke, Hampshire RG21 6XS.

Palgrave Macmillan in the US is a division of St Martin's Press LLC, 175 Fifth Avenue, New York, NY 10010.

Palgrave Macmillan is the global academic imprint of the above companies and has companies and representatives throughout the world.

Palgrave® and Macmillan® are registered trademarks in the United States, the United Kingdom, Europe and other countries.

ISBN 978–0–230–36974–0

This book is printed on paper suitable for recycling and made from fully managed and sustained forest sources. Logging, pulping and manufacturing processes are expected to conform to the environmental regulations of the country of origin.

A catalogue record for this book is available from the British Library.

A catalog record for this book is available from the Library of Congress.

10  9  8  7  6  5  4  3  2  1
21  20  19  18  17  16  15  14  13  12

Printed and bound in Great Britain by
CPI Antony Rowe, Chippenham and Eastbourne

*For my clever and elegant wife, Alison
and my charming and handsome son, Benedict*

# Contents

# List of Figures and Tables

## Figures

## Tables

# Preface

I really enjoy scribbling. Good thing, I suppose, as I am an academic and that is part of the job description. But being an extrovert (who speak before they think in order to find out what they are thinking), I enjoy writing to find out what I really think about issues. I hear odd phrases that attract my attention and note them down. Then, in an airport lounge or on the beach, I get them out and ponder what they mean. These may result in the sort of 800–1,000-word essays that appear in this book. This explains, partly, why they are a little quirky. Most are about the odd ideas that float about in offices around the topic of what one might loosely call work psychology.

I also enjoy reading, but that is a bit of a busman's holiday for an academic. I don't read novels, but business magazines ... and I even enjoy trashy management and self-help books, mainly when I'm travelling. They are a source of amusement and interest.

When people find out you are a psychologist there are a number of typical reactions. Some people walk away immediately, believing you are going to perceive or even perhaps expose some hidden secret, weakness or foible. Others challenge you by claiming, somewhat defensively, that isn't psychology/psychiatry just pure unscientific bunkum, dangerously misleading pseudo-science or only common sense? It's not worth an argument, so best to retreat ... which, after all, was probably their aim.

The third reaction is to try to get free advice about some personal issue considered to be psychological: about their partner or child, or some peculiarity they think they have. I have been asked "Why do I believe I have pretty feet?" and "What is the best way to prepare for going to the dentist?" You certainly encounter some odd questions, which get you thinking about how others see and experience the world.

This book is about talent and the lack of it. It is also about some of the ideas people have regarding the world of management. Some of these pieces have appeared in different guises in newspaper columns, magazine articles and motivational speeches.

I have, as always, various people to thank for their assistance and support. Andrew Lynch, my editor on *The Sunday Times*, has always been kind and helpful. John Taylor and David Pendleton have often given me good ideas. But, of course, and as always, it is Alison who gives me the best feedback. She uses what psychobabblers call *tough love*: that means giving it to me straight. If an idea is unsound, the style turgid and faltering, the logic weak ... or the topic simply boring, I get to know pretty fast and pretty clearly. Call it peer feedback or whatever, it was Alison who told me this joke: "Question: 'What is the difference between your wife and a terrorist?' Answer: 'You can negotiate with a terrorist!'" At our wedding anniversary lunch every September, which she lovingly calls my annual appraisal, I am given a robust strengths and weaknesses audit, in the vain hope, I suppose, that I might improve.

As always, all infelicitous phrasing, downright libellous accusations, factual inaccuracies and errors of judgment that appear in the book are mine alone.

ADRIAN FURNHAM

# Introduction

*If you want one year of prosperity, grow grain; ten years, grow trees; one hundred years, grow people.*

Chinese proverb

You can't have escaped noticing that "*talent management*" has become a fashionable, Human Resource (HR) buzzword (Gladwell 2002; Martin and Schmidt 2010) – well, "new-ish": buzzwords don't last for ever, and this one may be nearing its sell-by date. Is there anything new in the idea (Silzer and Church 2009)?

In some organizations the Personnel Department (which then became the HR Department) has been renamed the "*Talent Management Department*" (Economist Intelligence Unit 2006). Does that mean everyone is talented, thus making the concept redundant; or is there an equivalent Talentless Management Department who have, of course, a much more difficult task?

With bull markets there is a *war for talent*. Many assumed that there was an under-supply of talented people at all levels, and thus organizations were in a competitive battle to attract and retain, as well as develop, these special, but crucial, people who would ensure, they hoped, that the organization prospered. They were thought of as the new generation, who would be required to lead the organization into the future and ensure its survival.

At the time of writing, in a bear market, there is *a surfeit of talent; an over-supply*; and *wasted talent*. Yet it remains unclear *what talent actually is*; whether it needs special nurturing to last; and what it predicts. If talent is not merely a new name for an old construct or set of constructs, what does it comprise? And how does one develop a person into a talented manager?

There are various specific questions for those who are trying to assess and evaluate talent. Here are some issues and questions to ponder:

1. Write down all the synonyms and antonyms you can think of for "talent."
2. Have you ever worked with, or for, a really talented person? How did you know that person was talented? Describe your observations.

3. What are the lessons from the turnover of talented people? Why do talented people leave? Is this good or bad for them and/or your organization?
4. What processes would you put in place to recruit and select high fly-ers for your organization?
5. Should the list of those who are judged to be talented (or talentless) be kept secret? Indeed, could it ever become secret?
6. Under what circumstances should people who are labelled or nomi-nated as talented be taken off the list and others brought into the talent group? That is, what should be the nature of mobility for talented (and less talented) people?
7. Should you invest more or less time and money into the talent group than those not in this group? If the talented are in some way gifted, should employers not invest more in those who, for whatever reason, are seen to have less talent?
8. Imagine you have a budget of £5,000/$6,000 and three weeks in total (21 days) to develop your high flyers; what would you do?
9. Do you think it is a sign of being a really talented person that you could trust them to plan their own training and use your budget to realize their full potential?
10. What, in your view, are the three *easiest* and the three *hardest* things involved with talent management?

Which of these issues are you the most/least interested in or vexed by?

## Nine-box nonsense

Despite all the hype, the courses and the research-lite business books, most organizations still struggle with the most fundamental of questions: what is talent? How do you define talent, and therefore spot it? Can talent fade? Can ordinary people suddenly become talented?

It is seriously good to be in the talented group because the philosophy of most organizations seems to be "to him who hath, shall more be given." The talented receive more attention and more opportunities; in short, more time and money is spent on them. That is why people fight to get into the talent group: they are spoiled.

The talented also have one crucial advantage: *reputational head-starts*. These are sometimes, but not always, deserved. The fact that people know who you are, "one of the chosen," means many attribute to you positive features that lesser mortals don't receive.

There are, however, a number of problems attached to having a talent group or talent policy. The *first* is what to call those who are not gifted, talented or special. Are they second-rate, talentless or ordinary? Of course not; but what, then, are they to be labelled? This is why organizations choose names of colors or adopt metaphors for the haloed talent group. They are known as the "Gold Group" or "the Eagles." This approach never quite overcomes the problem, though. In airlines you fly first, business or traveller: not first, second and third class.

The *second* problem is the stability of talent: can it "go away," get used up, burnt out? This might mean the chosen ones who were once classified as talented later become reclassified, downgraded. Difficult for everybody, because it could imply an error of classification in the first place. So, it's rare. Once in, you stay there.

But it is the *third* issue that is probably the most problematic but not perceived to be so. Once the talented people have been found and deployed, the question then is about appraisal and promotion. What do you do with a talented engineer, finance manager or salesperson? Perhaps those whom the gods would destroy are first called talented?

The most common solution is the *nine-box category scheme*. This is based on two ratings: one of *performance* and the other of *potential* (see Figure I.1). The worst outcome is 1–1 (Box 1) – low performance and low potential; and the best is 3–3 (Box 9) – high on both ratings.

There are those most curious of mavericks, of course: the 1–3s or the 3–1s. The former are low on performance but high on potential. But why? Lazy folk? Badly managed? Not found their feet? A desert plant waiting for the wet season? Or what about great performance but no potential? Reached their level of incompetence? Stuck in a rut? Possessing a skill set that isn't needed any more?

There are numerous issues with the deployment of the nine-box grid. But without a doubt the most important is *who* does the rating and on what *database*. For more senior personnel the scoring is usually carried out by a senior HR manager and some board level management who meet to discuss the merits of the candidate for classification. They may be well-intentioned, but the problems are enormous.

Take the easier of the two ratings: performance. Performance on what? Delivering revenue targets, staff engagement or a change in management ability? All their competencies on a sort of aggregated score, or just their

**The performance / promotability matrix**

| Performance | High | Average | Low |
|---|---|---|---|
| **High** | ⑨ **Highly promotable**, has significant leadership potential. Exceptional performer – exceeds talented requirements. | ⑥ **Promotable** – at least one level. Exceptional talented performer – exceeds requirements. | ③ **At appropriate level.** Exceptional performer – exceeds requirements. |
| **Average** | ⑧ **Very promotable**, significant potential. Very effective performer – fully meets requirements. | ⑤ **Promotable** – probably at least one level. Very effective performer – fully meets requirements. | ② **At appropriate level.** Effective performer – meets requirements. |
| **Low** | ⑦ **Has potential to be highly promotable.** Partially meets requirements but needs training, mentoring, coaching. | ④ **Has potential to be promoted** – at least one level. Partially meets requirements. Needs improvement (new in current position). | ① **Somewhat over promoted.** Partially meets requirements. Needs significant improvement. |

Promotability

*Figure 1.1* Performance/promotability matrix

targets for this year? And who does the rating: boss, peers, subordinates or the individuals themselves? The boss has less information, and of a different type than the subordinates.

Frequently bosses have only two types of evidence: reputational data and productivity data. Staff know about competence, emotional intelligence and the like, while peers know about ambition, values and so on.

So the question is, who rates performance? Easy, of course, if there is something measureable, like money, but so much work is less tangible and team-based that it is very difficult to count, so measure ratings have to be made.

Performance ratings need to be conducted by the people who have the data. They need to be trained in rating. And they need to be trained in giving feedback.

But what about rating a person's potential? Potential for what? The next-level job? Strategic thinking? Ability to lead change? Innovation? Even if you were to rate all the above, and more, what are the data like?

What is a *high potential person*? There must be some simple, ubiquitous, but fundamentally important criteria. They need to be bright enough to learn new things and master increasingly technical briefs. They need to be ambitious and confident enough to want promotion. They need to be tough and resilient enough to cope with the stress that the job will bring. They need to be hard-working, conscientious and driven enough to take on the added burden. And perhaps they need to be persuasive, diplomatic and charming too.

At least the above unpacks the slippery "potential" category. It should encourage more reliable and more valid ratings, but again only by those who have the data.

The nine-box category system is crude and clumsy. As things operate at the time of writing, it benefits those who spend more effort on managing up and "reputation management" than on doing a good job.

## The fundamental questions

From a management perspective there seem to be a number of important questions:

- *Attracting talent*: This involves the recruitment of talented people, identifying the best methods to assess it and finding ways to persuade talented people to join the organization. This is essentially a *recruiting and selection task*. This may mean trying to attract people from universities as well as various firms. The aim is to make these especially (and perhaps unusually) talented people favorably disposed to your organization so that they apply for advertised positions. You have to ask (and answer) this question: why would any talented person want to come and work for you?

- *Developing talent*: One of the concepts associated with talent is the idea of the *potential* to rise up the organization to ever more important and challenging jobs. For this, it is thought (even) talented people require particular training, coaching or mentoring. This can, and should, be done on an individual basis as well as on a corporate level through leadership development, succession planning to new job integration and an assimilation initiative.
- *Retaining talent*: This involves keeping talented people once they have been selected. It involves understanding their particular and specific "package" and training needs. They might be motivated differently than less talented groups, and the task is to find how to keep them both happy *and* productive. This question addresses whether they need anything different compared to good management practices and equitable rewards to ensure they stay working for the organization. The issue is one of return on investment: on knowing how to turn a talented employee, into a talented manager, into a talented director and then, even a talented CEO.
- *Transferring talent:* Inevitably, talented people move – they move up the organization (almost by definition); they move to sister companies; they may head up overseas divisions of the company. Furthermore, they leave the organization. It is important to ensure that all issues associated with out-placement, relocation and retirement are done well.

These are all related to the management of talent. Robinson *et al.* (2009) suggest asking some simple questions:

- Does this person consistently exhibit our company values, support our mission, and enhance our culture?
- Does this person's performance consistently exceed expectations?
- Does this person's current behavior consistently align with the High Potential Indicators?

If the answer is affirmative, create an action plan to accelerate readiness for advancement, and identify challenging opportunities to test and develop capabilities.

## Definitions

Talent management, however, follows talent-spotting and selection. It is therefore extremely important to have a clear, specific and evidence-based definition of the concept of talent so as to know what to look for. Yet, despite the increasing number of books written about this topic, the concept remains unclear.

Talent is, quite simply, not a psychological concept. One approach is to list possible synonyms for talent and talented. These include: blessed; exceptional; experienced; flair; genius; giftedness; high potential; precocious; prodigy; superstar; wonderkid or *Wunderkind*. It is really only "giftedness" that has had any serious academic investigation.

Talent implies the possibility of people becoming more than they are. Silzer and Church (2009) argue that the concept of potential (talent) is all about something existing only in the realm of possibility. It is singular, immutable and context independent, or defined by and brought out only in certain situations. They note that high potential can be defined by role, level, breadth, record, strategic position or strategic area. The two authors analyzed 11 companies' definitions of talent/high potential and found evidence of six categories, variously defined:

- *Cognitive*: Cognitive ability/complexity, intelligence, navigates ambiguity, breadth of perspective, judgment, insightful, strategic reasoning, tactical problem solving.
- *Personality*: Dominance, sociability, stability, interpersonal, emotionally intelligent, authentic, optimistic, personal maturity, respect for people, self-aware, integrity.
- *Learning*: Adaptability, versatility, learning agility, receptive to feedback, eager to learn, flexible, seeks feedback, learns from mistakes.
- *Leadership*: Competent, inspiring, develops others, brings out the best in people, influential, challenges the status quo.
- *Motivation*: Drive, aspiration, engagement, initiative, energy, risk-taking, power/control, tenacity, passion for results, courage to take risks, commitment to company/impact.

- *Performance*: Leadership experience.
- *Other things*: Technical skills, culture fit, promotability, business knowledge/acumen.

They rather cleverly divide these groups into three categories: foundational dimensions (cognitive and personality); growth dimensions (learning and motivation); and career dimensions (leadership, performance and knowledge values). But, they argue, many questions remain to be answered regarding building a comprehensive model of potential that works for all organizations; deciding on clear criteria to enable people to reach their potential; and the problems of self-fulfilling prophesies in this area.

## Development

There are many ways to develop talent. Talented leaders provide much the same narrative of the factors that influenced them the most. Studies across organizations in different sectors as well as those within big corporations and across different corporate and national cultures, or even different historical time zones, reveal a similar story. Talented leaders mention six powerful learning experiences.

### Early work experience

This may be a "part-time" job while at school; a relatively unskilled summer holiday job during time at university; or one of the first jobs they ever had. For some it was the unadulterated tedium or monotony that motivated them powerfully never to repeat the experience. For others it was a particular work style or process that they had retained all their lives. This is something to look out for in the selection process.

### Working with other people

It is nearly always an immediate boss, but may be a colleague or one of the serious grown-ups; this person is almost always remembered as either very bad or very good, but both teach lessons. The message from this form of development perspective is to find a series of excellent role-model, mentor-type bosses for the talent group.

### Short-term assignments

Project work, standing in for another, or interim management. Because this takes people out of their comfort zone and exposes them to issues and problems they have never previously confronted, they learn quickly. For some it is the lucky break: serendipity provides an opportunity to discover a new skill or passion.

### First major line assignment

This is often the first promotion, foreign posting or departmental move to a higher position. It is frequently cited, because suddenly the stakes had become higher, everything was more complex, novel and ambiguous. There were more pressures; the buck stopped here. Suddenly the difficulties of management became real, and you were accountable. The idea, then, is to develop appropriate "stretch assignments" for talented people as soon as they are appointed.

### Hardships of various kinds

This is about attempting to cope in a crisis, which may be professional or personal. It teaches the real value of things – technology, loyal staff, a supportive head office. The experiences are those of battle-hardened soldiers, or the "been there, done that" brigade. Hardship teaches many lessons: how resourceful and robust some people can be, and how others panic and cave in. It teaches some to admire a fit and happy organization when they see it. It teaches them to distinguish needs and wants. It teaches a little about minor forms of post-traumatic stress disorder, and the virtues of stoicism, hardiness and a tough mental attitude.

### Management development

Some remember and quote their MBA experience; far fewer mention some specific (albeit fiendishly expensive) course. One or two quote the experience of receiving 360° feedback. More recall a coach, either because that person was so good, or so awful. This is bad news for trainers, business school teachers and coaches.

To the extent that leadership is acquired, developed and learned, rather than "gifted," it is achieved mainly through experiences at work. Inevitably some experiences are better than others because they teach different lessons in different ways. Some people apparently acquire these valuable experiences despite, rather than as a result of, company policy. Experiential learning takes time, but timing is important. It's not a steady, planned accumulation of insights and skills. Some experiences teach very little, or even inculcate bad habits.

But three factors conspire to defeat the experiential model. *First*, both young managers and their bosses want to short-circuit experience: learn faster, cheaper, better. Hence the appeal of the one-minute manager, the one-day MBA and the short course. *Second*, many HR professionals see this approach as disempowering them, because they are "in charge" of the leadership development programme. *Third*, some see experience as a test, not a developmental exercise.

Perhaps leadership potential and talent should be defined as *the ability to learn from experience*. Equally, every move, promotion or challenge should also be assessed from the point of view of its learning potential.

Approaching the issue somewhat differently, Martin and Schmidt (2010) offer various suggestions of ways to develop talent: emphasize future competencies; place people on "intense assignments" (not functional and business rotations); assign rising stars to the riskiest and most challenging jobs; create a development plan for each of them; re-evaluate top talent annually; give them special recognition programmes; monitor their progress; and have open, honest discussions and emphasize how their plans fit in with company plans.

## Retention

One important current concern is talent retention. Martin and Schmidt (2010) argue that as many as a quarter of high-potential people in big American companies intend to "jump ship" within a year, and a fifth believe their personal aspirations are different from what the company has planned for them. They think that companies make six common mistakes in trying to manage the "talented":

1. Assuming they are all engaged when they are not, if they are not challenged, rewarded and recognized enough.
2. Mistaking current performance for high performance: not all are able to, or want to, step up to tougher roles.
3. Delegating talent development to line managers who may not be qualified to do the job.
4. Shielding talent from more difficult assignments where they will learn more.
5. Not offering them differentiated compensation and recognition from that offered to colleagues.
6. Keeping them in the dark with respect to what is planned for them.

Bad management, Martin and Schmidt (2010) argue, leads to three problem types: *engaged dreamers* (people with aspirations, but who don't quite have the required ability); *disengaged stars* (people not really committed to the organization); and *misaligned stars* (who aren't prepared to make the real sacrifices required).

## Giftedness in children

There is an extensive literature on gifted children, which is consistent in what it highlights (Brody 2005; Brody and Mills 2005; Gagne 2004; Heller *et al.* 1993; Shavinina 2004). This, therefore, is a good place to begin to define talent. Research on gifted children tends to highlight the following characteristics:

- Excel at *memory* activities beyond what one would expect at the given age level.
- Demonstrate unusually *mature thinking* on tasks that are complicated; learn very quickly new information or ways of doing things, or perceive hidden meanings.
- Show *advanced understanding* or precocious development of a specific skill area – for example, early reading or mathematics – without having been directly instructed, or rapid development when provided the opportunity in the arts.
- Show *self-management* of their own learning.
- Have a high need for a *variety of experiences*; seek new and different opportunities to investigate and seem to delight in novel problems to solve.
- Seek *older children* as playmates and engage in especially creative imaginative play scenarios.
- Have an *advanced vocabulary* and enjoy playing with words or other means of symbolically representing in their world.
- Demonstrate notable *variability* between very sophisticated thinking and behavior in other ways that indicates they are still young children.

There seem to be three or four distinct clusters of characteristics. The first is both general and specific *ability*. Thus gifted children are described as being observant, inquisitive, smart. They learn quickly, have a big vocabulary and enjoy intellectual challenges. They are also well co-ordinated, dextrous, athletic and energetic (that is, have advanced psychomotor skills). They can also show impressive visual, spatial and auditory skills. Perhaps it is their advanced vocabulary that most clearly marks them out as different.

Second, gifted children are known for their *creative thinking*. They are innovators, improvisers, independent and original thinkers. They enjoy coming up with several solutions to standard problems. They also do not mind standing out from a crowd. Unlike adults, they are uninhibited about their creative products and express interest and confidence in the process.

Third, highly gifted children appear to have higher levels of *social intelligence*. They are expressive, self-confident, popular and able. They show good social judgment and are able to foresee the consequences and implications of their judgments. They often assume responsibility in social settings, which is accepted by others. In this sense they get elected to positions of leadership by both their peers and their teachers.

Finally, they tend to have higher levels of task commitment. They are able to concentrate easily. Often they also show other characteristics, such as assuming task leadership roles in situations as well as demonstrating advanced psychomotor coordination and visual perception.

Not all gifted children grow up to be talented adults and vice versa, but it does seem that this is a rich source of hypotheses from which to consider the dimension of talent in adults.

There is in the gifted child literature one other important theme: *the cost of giftedness*. As well as the immense benefits of being gifted, researchers have pointed to disadvantages and drawbacks. Three are often mentioned:

- Raised expectations of others – it is clear why this occurs, but can put pressure on gifted children always to excel, everywhere and in every task. Lack of achievement can be seen erroneously as laziness. This has implications as to whether organizations are wise to "anoint" people into a "high flyer" group.
- Perfectionism – it has been noticed that some gifted children show signs of perfectionistic obsessionality. This trait can slow down the rate of their performance and leads to both anxiety and depression. Perfectionists set themselves too high a target in all they do, but often fail to achieve such targets and hence feel dejected because of their failure.

- Self-doubt – it is indeed paradoxical that gifted children can show considerable self-doubt. This may be caused by the implicit and explicit expectations others (especially parents and teachers) have of them, and which they feel they cannot easily fulfil. It may also be caused by the feeling that they always have to excel at everything that is demanding.

There is an "adult version" of these problems in successful (if not gifted, then talented) adults that can be described as the *impostor syndrome*. The characteristics of this are that the successful person, often suddenly propelled into the limelight in the arts or business, feels like a fake – an impostor not worthy of the accolade or deserving of success. As a result, the person tends to discount his or her success by attributing it to luck, chance and circumstances. Indeed they tend to become fearful of success, because they see it as causing problems for themselves. The strategy many apply is self-handicapping, which prevents them from failing, perhaps through drink, drugs or illegal activities. They feel strongly the need to reduce the pressure not to fail. This is the dark side of giftedness and talent.

It seems, then, that industrial and organizational (I-O) psychologists may have overlooked the gifted child literature, which offers considerable empirical and theoretical insight into the concept of talent.

However interesting these definitions are, there is a fundamental problem with relying too heavily on the gifted children literature. The issue is both a surprise and a disappointment. It is quite simply that studies that have traced gifted children from their early identification and thence through into adulthood have shown that a surprisingly large number lead very ordinary, not particularly successful or outstanding lives.

This raises the question of the role of ability over other things, such as personality, and particularly motivation. While it is not that difficult to measure personality, the measurement of motivation (to do well, succeed, be a CEO) remains seriously problematic.

## The requirements of leaders

Every organization understands that it needs to recruit and retain talented leaders for the future. This is particularly true for managers of a multicultural workforce in an age of globalization (Vijver 2008). A central question of this quest is to know what one is looking for, and second, how to assess or measure it. Five factors come up repeatedly.

## Cognitive ability

The single best predictor of leadership/management success is intelligence, particularly at higher levels of management. This is not to be confused with formal education, though they are modestly related. Managers need to be *bright enough*; that is, they require some minimum level of intelligence to do the job well. As one goes up the organizational hierarchy jobs become more complex. Further, things can change or need to be changed, and leaders have to understand those issues. They need to spot future trends. Bright people are curious.

Followers like, respect and support brighter leaders. Brighter leaders are both seen as, and are, more effective than less bright leaders. Brighter leaders are better at transforming organizations and managing change. Brighter managers have more (intellectual) self-confidence and suffer less stress. Brighter leaders learn faster, are more positive about personal growth, and are more adaptable. The present-day fear of IQ testing has made intelligence a taboo topic, but it remains fundamentally important.

## Emotional adjustment and stability

Senior management and leadership positions always involve stress. Amen. People have to make hard decisions, take risks, face criticism and setbacks. They need to be hardy and resilient to take the pace and challenges of modern business life.

Less stable people are, in essence, prone to neuroses. Unstable people tend to be tense, touchy and thin-skinned. They can have rapidly fluctuating moods, and be very brittle. Unstable, less hardy people are prone to anxiety and depression. They are particularly vulnerable to stress and stress-related illness. Neurosis is related to absenteeism. Unstable people can be self-pitying, self-defeating and prone to a depressive, gloomy outlook. Followers report having considerable difficulty with the moodiness and vulnerability of unstable managers.

Stable, well-adjusted managers, by contrast, cope well under inevitable periods of stress. Stable leaders tend to have healthy, adaptable coping strategies, whereas the opposite is true for their less able colleagues. Stable managers are also more optimistic.

## The work ethic and conscientiousness

Talented managers need to be hard-working and self-disciplined. They have to be dependable, reliable and responsible. They need to be responsive to various stakeholders – their staff, colleagues, customers and shareholders. They have to be efficient and organized. They need to understand the need to plan ahead and to ensure that things are always done to the required standard.

Conscientiousness is closely related to competence, which is one of the highest-rated virtues followers want in their managers. Conscientiousness is also related to dedication, deliberation and dutifulness. Conscientious managers are hard-working, but they learn to work smart as well as to put in long hours. They understand when and why they need to go the extra mile. Conscientious leaders tend to be achievement-oriented and aspirational for themselves and others.

Conscientious managers deliver on their promises, which are realistic, and they tend to follow ethical rules sensibly and sensitively. They are true to their word: they "pitch up and pitch in"; they pull their weight; they don't shirk responsibility. That is important. Hard work can make up for a lot of sins.

## Emotional intelligence, social skills and charm

Management is a social activity; a participant and contact sport. Leaders have to inspire and support their staff. They are in the motivation business. In essence, emotional intelligence involves understanding and the ability to influence other people. But it also involves self-understanding or awareness and the knowledge of how to deal with people's mood and frailties. Emotional intelligence is essentially about having social skills, charm and insight. Emotionally intelligent managers understand the importance and power of emotions in everyday life. They are good at the emotional regulation of daily life.

We know that emotionally intelligent leaders are liked, trusted and admired by their staff. Managers with high emotional quotient (EQ) always get the best out of their staff and are hence highly productive. High EQ leaders are particularly successful in difficult times, when organizations are under considerable pressure. High EQ leaders understand the psychological needs of their key staff members and excel at getting the best out of them. Emotional intelligence is linked to being more assertive, empathic, optimistic and self-motivated.

## *Motivation, drive, the need to achieve*

Motivation is the engine of managerial success, but it needs direction. People are quite clearly motivated by different things – power, influence, control, recognition. The great problem with the concept of motivation is that it appears at the same time to be all-encompassing, yet very vague.

People are motivated to achieve a goal: the more motivated they are, the more time, effort and energy they will be willing to put into achieving that goal. More important, most of these goals are not easily satisfied, and this motivation does not stop once they have been achieved. This is true of both psychological goals, such as recognition, and more objective goals such as monetary reward.

We know that all employees are motivated to seek recognition and reward from those they work for, to boost their self-esteem. Motivated leaders are often particularly sensitive to issues around fairness – that is, that reward is directly related to effort, that input and output are closely linked. Motivated leaders have realistic expectations, and set for themselves and others attainable but stretching goals. Motivated leaders are less distracted by setbacks. They learn from their mistakes and direct their efforts most efficiently.

## Reviews and speculations

The expectations and lifestyle of people in the West is changing, and businesses have to take that into consideration in both talent-spotting and management. There is the perception of a marketplace of talent: a limited pool of individuals whose talent is portable and transferable across corporate and national boundaries. Further, those talented people are seen as having specific characteristics (creativity, drive, energy, insight) to help companies both survive and thrive.

The Economist Intelligence Unit (2006) produced a case study report that showed that chief executive officers (CEOs) as well as HR managers are spending more of their time (around 25 percent) engaged with talent management, because this is believed to drive corporate performance, even though its impact is hard to measure. The CEOs see this process as identifying and grooming talented individuals at all levels to enable them to rise more quickly up the corporate ladder. Performance evaluations and assessment/developmental center reports provide the data to decide on programs, projects and relocations which provide the experience to test and train (and unleash) the talent.

Many believe that talent management is a source, often a major source, of competitive advantage. Talented leaders enhance productivity, supposedly through a high performance culture. It needs little more than getting the right people in the top places. It is seen inevitably as both a selector/assessment and a training/mentoring activity, and is inevitably caught up with all the issues around successful management. It is often seen as carrying out accelerated leadership development with highly selected individuals. In short, it is identifying the CEOs of the future.

*The Economist* report notes that "a rigorous approach to obtaining reliable performance data is essential" (p. 11), but, as ever, there is little indication of *what* to measure and *how*. Far too much reliance appears to be put on company appraisal scheme data and not enough on psychometrically proven assessment and developmental centre data.

A Deloitte Research Study on talent by Athey (2008) also covers much of this ground. Thus, she argues, CEOs are worried about the dwindling supply of talent, the problem of their "star talent" being poached by the opposition, and (paradoxically) that when they poach others, the newcomers rarely perform as hoped. The demographic time-bomb worries them, as do education systems and evidence of growing employee disengagement.

Athey (2008) presented a fairly standard four-stage model – acquire, deploy, develop and retain talent. Curiously, relatively little is said about acquiring talent, which seems to be the fundamental process. Much more is said about the developmental process – to give talented people educational experiences. The "deploy" part is particularly interesting and important. It has three components: (i) identify the "deep-rooted" skills, interests and knowledge of the individual; (ii) find their best fit in the organization; and (iii) craft the job design and conditions that help them to perform. This is a particularly interesting idea, though not fully explored. It is the notion of not only finding the super-adaptive and flexible individual, but also making sure the organization is adaptive enough to match the profile of the individual.

Part of this plan is to ensure that the corporate culture helps the process. Thus *command and control* should be replaced by *trust and respect*. Win–lose must be replaced by a connected and collaborative culture. The concept is that talented people are attracted to companies where employees are aligned, and capable and committed, and therefore (one hopes!) productive.

# The psychology of high flyers

Usually, the definition of a high flyer is a talented individual capable of taking on increasingly senior and more responsible jobs. High flyers' talent is shown in their ability to adapt, learn fast and cope with complex tasks, whether in the public or private sector. When people are asked to evaluate and assess young (or not so young) people at an assessment centre for selection, promotion or succession management reasons, the "top" category usually refers to a small group of high flyers who supposedly can "make it to the top", implying that they can reach board or CEO level.

Naturally, there has been a great deal of speculation over a long period of time as to the characteristics these very special people manifest. Cox and Cooper (1988) identified "key personal characteristics" that were related to success. These were:

- *Determination*: a characteristic often derived from childhood experiences where they had to take personal responsibility for themselves.
- *Learning from adversity*: using adversity and setbacks to develop better coping strategies and learn new skills.
- *Seizing chances*: not the same as opportunism, but enthusiastically taking very difficult decisions early in life.
- *Being achievement oriented*: being ambitious and positive, and seeking long-term big prizes.
- *Internal locus of control*: being a self-confident instrumentalist, not a passive fatalist.
- *Having a well-integrated value system:* having a clear, integrated and lived-by value system (valuing integrity, independence, initiative and so on).
- *Effective risk management*: moderate, but calculated, risk takers.
- *Having clear objectives*: having both long- and short-term objectives and striving constantly to reach them.
- *Dedication to the job:* feeling the job was the most important aspect of life yet not being a workaholic.
- *Intrinsic motivation*: finding energy and enthusiasm in the job itself; not simply being motivated by extrinsic reward.
- *Well-organized lifestyle*: this prevents conflicts between work and home life.
- *A pragmatic rather than an intellectual approach*: having practical interests and pursuits rather than intellectual ones.

- *Analytic and problem-solving skills*: perhaps seeming intuitive rather than rational.
- *Exemplary people skills*: being socially skilled, open and consultative; but also being authoritative.
- *Being innovative*: not being constrained by procedures, current systems and assumptions.
- *Having a competitive, hard-driving lifestyle*: sometimes called the type A lifestyle.

Cox and Cooper noted:

> One quality which does seem to be universal among high flyers is *resilience* and the ability not only to cope with but also to learn from adversity. This characteristic is a function of their strong *internal locus of control*, aided by a clear *value system* and strong *self concept*. In other words, people who reach the top are clear about *who they are* and *what they believe in*. This aspect of personality is strongly influenced by early experience, and so, probably has to be considered as a quality required at the selection stage, rather than as something which can be trained by the organisation. Even so, some development can possibly be offered through the medium of such activities as 'outward bound' programmes, which certainly aid in the development of the capacity to overcome adversity, and do often force individuals to confront their assumptions about themselves and their values. Sensitive and skilled mentoring can also aid this process. (1988, p. 147)

McCall and colleagues have attempted to identify executive potential, or executive competences, also known as end state skills (McCall 1998; McCall *et al.* 1990; Spreitzer *et al.* 1997). To a large extent this team argues that the ability to learn from experience is the fundamental key to managerial potential. They argue that a review of the diverse literature on the early identification of executive success through the assessment centre literature indicates five themes or areas of importance:

1. *General intelligence*: simple IQ or cognitive ability has a clear connection to business-related issues such as analytical agility, reasoning, incisiveness, and synthetic and visionary thinking.
2. *Business knowledge*: this is an understanding of the company's and sector's products, markets and policies as well as a breadth of awareness and interest in trends across the market as a whole.

3. *Interpersonal skills*: social skills are important in handling relation-ships, team building, the capacity to motivate and inspire, as well as to align people behind particular strategies.
4. *Commitment*: this can be expressed in various ways – for example, a passion for success, personal drive and perseverance. They all refer to extreme interest in, and commitment to, work.
5. *Courage*: to a large extent this means being non-risk-averse and will-ing to take action to ensure that things happen. It is related to self-confidence, but not arrogance.

A theme identified strongly by this team is the ability to learn from experience. Those with potential take a proactive approach to learning, they learn from their mistakes and adapt well to difficult circumstances as well as seeking and using feedback to make sense of their work environment.

In later work, McCall *et al.* (1995) identified eleven dimensions he believes relate to being a high flyer:

1. **Seeks opportunities to learn.** Has demonstrated a pattern of learn-ing over time. Seeks out experiences that may change perspective or provide an opportunity to learn new things. Takes advantage of oppor-tunities to do new things when such opportunities come along. Has developed new skills and has changed over time.
2. **Acts with integrity.** Tells the truth and is described by others as honest. Is not self-promoting, and consistently takes responsibility for his or her actions.
3. **Adapts to cultural differences.** Enjoys the challenge of working in and experiencing cultures different from his or her own. Is sensitive to cultural differences, works hard to understand them, and changes behavior in response to them.
4. **Is committed to making a difference.** Demonstrates a strong com-mitment to the success of the organisation and is willing to make per-sonal sacrifices to contribute to that success. Seeks to have a positive impact on the business. Shows passion and commitment through a strong drive for results.
5. **Seeks broad business knowledge.** Has an understanding of the business that goes beyond his or her own limited area. Seeks to under-stand both the products or services and the financial aspects of the business. Seeks to understand how the various parts of the business fit together.

6. **Brings out the best in people.** Has a special talent with people that is evident in his or her ability to pull people together into highly effective teams. Is able to work with a wide variety of people, drawing the best out of them and achieving consensus in the face of disagreement.

7. **Is insightful: sees things from new angles.** Other people admire this person's intelligence, particularly his or her ability to ask insightful questions, identify the most important part of a problem or issue, and see things from a different perspective.

8. **Has the courage to take risks.** Will take a stand when others disagree, go against the status quo, persevere in the face of opposition. Has the courage to act when others hesitate and will take both personal and business risks.

9. **Seeks and uses feedback.** Pursues, responds to, and uses feedback. Actively asks for information on his or her impact and has changed as a result of such feedback.

10. **Learns from mistakes.** Is able to learn from mistakes. Changes direction when the current path isn't working, responds to data without getting defensive, and starts over after setbacks.

11. **Is open to criticism.** Handles criticism effectively: does not act threatened or get overly defensive when others (especially superiors) are critical.

The high flyer approach, however, has fundamental problems, the greatest of which is the identification of such people in the first place. The criteria for being considered a high flyer are rarely explicit or agreed upon consensually. Worse still, it is not unusual for an identified high flyer to have a serious "fall to earth" not long after a study is complete. Given that the whole approach attempts to find out what is unique to the psyche of the high flyer, this is a fundamental issue.

Locke (1997) also devised a list of what can be called predictors of success:

- *Cognition*: reality focus; honesty; independence and self-confidence; active mind; competence/ability; vision.
- *Motivation*: egotistic passion for the work; commitment to action; ambition; effort and tenacity.
- *Attitude toward employees*: respect for ability; commitment to justice; rewarding merit.

Yet another opinion, as opposed to research, based list is set out in Table I.1.

While the lists are impressively long and fairly commonsensical they have the traditional drawbacks of such an approach. The data is based on self-report (interviews and questionnaires) and it may be that beliefs and behavior patterns are ignored or "repacked" to make them seem more attractive. Certainly many high flyers have a reputation for being egotistical, ruthless and amoral, though this is not how they present themselves to the world.

The lists are long, but not rank ordered. Are some characteristics more important than others? And if so, which? And what is the relationship between these different characteristics? How are they related? Can they be reduced to a more parsimonious and clearer list? Indeed, this is why the early trait approach to leadership failed: there was no agreement about, or good empirical evidence in support of, a parsimonious list of identical traits.

Jennings *et al.* (1994) reported numerous famous "elite entrepreneurs" (people who built and control companies) and "special entrepreneurs" (people who have worked their way up to the CEO position in organizations). These individuals may or may not be classified as talented or high flying.

*Table I.1*   Most and least important skills and attributes for effective leadership

| Ten *most* important characteristics of great leaders | Ten *least* important characteristics |
|---|---|
| Honesty and integrity at all times | Committed to all personal relationships |
| Clearly communicates expectations to all concerned | Thinks analytically |
| Recognises and rewards achievements | Always sensitive to others' needs |
| Adapts to all important changes | Has perseverance |
| Inspires others to work smarter and harder | Creates clear work plans and timetables for self and others |
| Puts the right people in the right positions at the right time | Breaks down all projects into manageable components |
| Has the passion to succeed | Has a strong commitment to people diversity |
| Identifies and articulates long-term vision for future for self and others | Properly manages relationships with third parties |
| Persuades and encourages others to move in desirable direction | Has years of experience in positions of management |
| Accepts personal responsibility for success or failure | Is original and creative |

*Source*: Adapted from Corporate Leadership Council (2001).

Jennings *et al.* examined early childhood experiences; socio-demographic origins; education; specific support from others; their approach to work and their work ethic; their personality traits and their philanthropic interests. The authors focused on three spheres of life/work – education and work history; personality with developmental history; and non-work/ family environment. Their results were surprisingly similar to the earlier study (Cox and Cooper 1988).

The method was retrospective and biographical. This is often the approach of historians. Borrowing heavily from other explanatory systems, Cox and Cooper (1988) also present a developmental model for managerial success. First, they note the importance both of parental attitudes and values but also early trauma associated with separation of one kind or another. Next, they did not find schooling at a primary, secondary or tertiary level was particularly influential or important. Indeed, the choice of institution may well reflect parental values, which are the really important issue. Early experience at work is seen to be most important, particularly having a helpful early mentor or model and succeeding when early "make-or-break" opportunities presented themselves. Their model is given in Table I.2.

According to Gunter and Furnham (2001), there are three major problems with the high flyer biographical method. The *first* is specifying what constitutes a high flyer. No single criterion suffices. Inevitably, luck and chance play a part, hence the particular characteristics that high

*Table I.2*    Factors contributing to high-flyer performance

| DEVELOPMENTAL EXPERIENCES | THE INDIVIDUAL | DETERMINANTS OF PERFORMANCE |
|---|---|---|
| *EARLY EXPERIENCE* Develops reliance on own resources, is achievement oriented, postpones gratification | *PARENT* Well integrated value system passed on to the child | *MANAGEMENT PHILOSOPHY –* Balanced work–life issues Tendency to be strict but fair |
| *EDUCATION* Helps develop cognitive, emotional and social skills | *ADULT* Very effective analysis and problem solving skills → | *MANAGEMENT SKILLS* Big picture People skills |
| *CAREER EXPERIENCE* Successful response to challenge, seek out and use opportunities | *CHILD* Shows enthusiasm, energy, commitment and focus | *MOTIVATION* Intrinsic rather than extrinsic leadership potential |

*Source*: Adapted from Cox and Cooper (1988).

flyers have may be little more than opportunity-spotting and exploiting entrepreneurial openings faster and more successfully than others. The business of defining a high flyer or a member of a successful business elite is by no means simple. Ideally, researchers would specify, objectively and explicitly, a range of criteria that would explain the principle by which certain people are included and others excluded from the sample.

The *second* problem is actually getting the nominated high flyers to take part in the study by agreeing to an interview or completing a survey. High flyers soon become "over-researched," and receive little personal benefit from participating. Hence many of those who have been carefully selected refuse to take part, which forces the researchers to weaken their criteria and indeed the study as a whole.

*Third*, these sorts of studies almost never have a control group of those matched on a number of criteria who simply did not "make it." Thus it is not really possible to say whether the special characteristics of high flyers identified by researchers are unique to them, or indeed played any part in their success.

## Talent derailment

Furnham (2003) spelled out a theory as to why talented people derail. He argued that the story of Icarus was a good example to help in understanding the syndrome. In Greek mythology, Icarus was the son of the inventor, Daedalus. Cretan King Minos locked the father and son up in a high tower. The talented Daedalus made two sets of wings out of feathers and wax, which they would use to escape; he told his son that the only "design fault" was that the wax might melt if they flew too close to the sun. Icarus ignored the good advice of his wise father, flew too high, melted his wings, crashed into the sea and drowned.

It is not clear from the myth precisely why Icarus disobeyed his father. Was he a sensation seeker prone to accidents? Did he do it out of boredom? Was he a disobedient, rebellious child? Was he simply beguiled by his own hubris?

We don't know the answers. Indeed, it is the function of myths and case studies that they allow for multiple interpretations. We do know that the modern derailed high-flier bears an uncanny resemblance to Icarus.

But how and why were they chosen? What did the assessors miss? Or did the problem arise in the way they were managed? There is a growing literature on management derailment and why it occurs, particularly in those once labelled as talented:

- *Aberrant (leaders)* This emphasizes abnormality, atypicality and deviance from the right or normal type. It has two themes: unusualness but also a departure from acceptable standards. That is, it has a statistical *and* a moral side to it.
- *Anti-social (leaders)* This echoes the immoral nature of leaders who can be anti-social in the way selfish people may be, but more likely in the way that delinquents are anti-social. And, more importantly, because perhaps it echoes the new term for a psychopathic condition: having an anti-social personality disorder.
- *Dark side (triad) (leaders)* This is to contrast the bright and the dark; the outside, the obvious and the straightforward with the inside, the obscure and the devious. Dark implies something that is evil, dismal and menacing. The triad suggests three separable constituents of evil.
- *Derailed (leaders)* This emphasizes the idea of being thrown off course. Trains derail from tracks. Leaders that were set fair in a particular direction deviate from the path and are unable to move forward. It is sometimes hyphenated with *deranged*, which implies not only a breakdown in performance but also into insanity.
- *Despotic (leaders)* This is taken from the historical literature emphasizing the misuse and abuse of power by oppressive, absolutist leaders. It highlights the autocratic type or style of leadership.
- *Destructive (leaders)* This is used by historians in this context to look at a particular leadership style; it speaks of the ruining, spoiling or neutralizing of a group or force led by a particular person.
- *Incompetent (leaders)* This is used to suggest inadequate, ineffective or unqualified. It implies the absence of something required rather than the presence of something not required. Incompetent leaders are ineffective because they are lacking in particular qualities.
- *Malignant (leaders)* These are leaders who spread malevolence, the opposite of benevolence. Malevolence is misconduct, doing harm such as maliciously causing pain or damage. Malignant leaders, like cancer, grow fast and are deadly.

- *Toxic (leaders)* This refers to the poisonous effect leaders have on all they touch. Toxic substances kill rather than repel. Again this refers to the consequences of a particular leadership style.
- *Tyrannical (leaders)* This refers to tyrants who show arbitrary, oppressive and unjust behavior. Tyrants tend to usurp power and then brutally oppress those they command.

Later Furnham (2007) argued that three categories or types of personality disorders and traits are most commonly implicated in management derailment: antisocial (psychopathic), narcissistic and histrionic. Machiavellianism (which is not strictly a personality disorder) has been considered as another dimension. These have been variously described as the dark triad of personality (Paulus and Williams 2002), though there is some disagreement about all the dimensions. In lay terms, psychopaths are selfish, callous, superficially charming, lacking empathy and remorse; narcissists are attention-seeking, vain, self-focused and exploitative; while Machiavellians are deceptive, manipulative and deeply self-interested.

Paradoxically, these disorders often prove to be an asset in acquiring and temporarily holding down senior management positions. The charm of the psychopath, the self-confidence of the narcissist, the clever deceptiveness of the Machiavellian and the emotional openness of the histrionic may be, in many instances, useful business traits. When candidates are physically attractive, well-educated, intelligent and have a dark triad profile it is not difficult to see why they are selected for senior positions in management. In this sense, assessors and selectors must bear part of the blame for not selecting out those who so often later derail so spectacularly. They do not recognize in the biography of the individual the crucial indicators of the disorder. Alternatively, the biography as portrayed in the CV might easily be a work of fiction.

The lay persons' image of a psychopath is often one of a dangerous mass murderer or perhaps an amazingly successful confidence trickster. Similarly, many would admire the self-confidence of the person with a narcissistic personality disorder. Further, the emotional lability and showiness of the histrionic personality-disordered manager in a creative job may result in them being rated as creative rather than disturbed. The clever deviousness of the Machiavellian may also be admired as an indication of toughness. In this sense, "mild" forms of these pathologies could appear generally or at specific times, which could be very advantageous to the manager.

## Strengths and weaknesses

Positive psychology in business has a new and beguiling message. The old-style, puritanical, work-on-your-weakness message is rejected. The reason is that this is a mistaken misallocation of energy and focus. It's difficult, if not impossible, to "correct," eliminate or conquer personal weaknesses, particularly among those who are older. The message is that you are let off the hook for your weaknesses – put them aside; ignore them. Rather, find and explore your strengths. Focus on what you are good at.

The "strengths" school urges you to find your strengths first. Next, to use those strengths; play to them. But could this lead to problems? Could the charismatic, inspirational leader rely too much on presentation and not enough on substance? People with great strengths may overuse them, misapply them or rely on them too much. Could determination become obstinacy? Integrity become zealotry and thoughtful analysis turn into paralysis? Celebrating one's new-found strengths may also make people less exploratory, change-oriented or eager to learn alternative approaches. They may focus on the past.

Should one really ignore one's weaknesses? Is there no point in working on them at all? What about learning and development? Surely the strengths-based philosophy suggests assigning people to tasks and areas of responsibility that allow them to use their strengths? They would be robbed of learning something new: developmental opportunities, a bigger picture, diversity of experience.

Working one's way to the top is about learning new ideas, approaches and skills as one "moves" through complexity. Ignoring weaknesses can excuse one from tackling necessary and important work. Big jobs require many skills and strengths. You can't just ignore the skills you don't have! The strengths approach can sound egocentric, self-indulgent and delusionally optimistic. Bizarrely, for such an upbeat creed it doesn't emphasize growth but use of what is already there.

Weaknesses left unchecked do damage. More important, it can seem simplistic to divide the world into these clear categories. Are there not many examples of people who have turned weaknesses (such as a physical handicap) into their greatest strength – stutterers who become great orators; the Helen Kellers of this world?

But more of the many studies on management derailment show that great strengths overused, misapplied but over-abundant, can in fact be great weaknesses. Where is the line between high self-esteem and self-confidence and clinical narcissism? Where is the line between care-ful, rule-following meticulousness and perfectionistic obsessive compul-siveness? Where is the line between colorful, dynamic and vivacious and having a narcissistic personality disorder?

Certainly, the strengths-based message about maximizing your innate gifts is correct. But a few *ifs* here: if you have a number of strengths rel-evant to your job; if you are prepared to learn new skills; if you also work on those things you have to do which you are not so good at; and if you do not become an arrogant over-user of the talents you have. Hubris leads to nemesis. Few great leaders have not known what they are good at, but they have also learned to put in the necessary work and effort to develop other skills and techniques that did not "come as easily."

Consider the list in Table I.3.

Which of these strengths are most important in a talented leader? Which can easily be overused to reveal a weakness? Which are most desir-able to have but will not do you any good in the business world?

## Management failure

It is said that a psychologist going through a famous university library in the late 1980s found 400 books on depression and only two on happiness which provoked him into trying to fill the gap. Psychologists seemed to assume that if you didn't have depression you were happy, and that this seemingly trivial subject did not merit research time and effort.

This was all before the positive psychology revolution and the shock-ing discovery to economists that wealth was very weakly related to health, happiness and well-being. Today, happiness is a serious topic for research.

Now, if you look at the more than 50,000 publications with *leadership* in their title, there is an equal conspiracy of neglect. There are autobio-graphical and biographical studies of leaders, there are "how to" books in droves, and there are scholarly works developing theories about the topic. There are studies of wicked, evil leaders, often written by histori-ans and occasionally psychiatrists, but almost nothing on *Wunderkinder.* It appears to be a taboo subject akin to mental and physical illness in the nineteenth century, and homosexuality in the twentieth century. It is not that we refuse to admit that it happens, but nobody is prepared to talk about it.

*Table I.3*   Personal strengths

1. **Curiosity**: interest in, intrigued by many things
2. **Love of learning**: knowing more, reading, understanding
3. **Good judgment**: critical thinking, rationality, open-mindedness
4. **Ingenuity**: originality, practical intelligence, street-smart
5. **Social intelligence**: emotional/personal intelligence, good with feelings
6. **Wisdom**: seeing the big picture, having perspective
7. **Bravery**: courage, valor, fearlessness
8. **Persistence**: perseverance, diligence, industriousness
9. **Integrity**: honesty, genuineness, truthful
10. **Kindness**: generosity, empathetic, helpful
11. **Loving**: able to love and be loved; deep sustained feelings
12. **Citizenship**: team worker, loyalty, duty to others
13. **Fairness**: moral valuation, equality and equity
14. **Leadership**: able to motivate groups, inclusive, focused
15. **Self-control**: able to regulate emotions, non-impulsive
16. **Prudence**: cautious, far-sighted, deliberative, discreet
17. **Humility**: modest, unpretentious, humble
18. **Appreciative of beauty**: seeking excellence, experience of awe/wonder
19. **Gratitude**: thankful, grateful
20. **Optimism**: hopefulness, future-mindedness, positive
21. **Spirituality**: faith, philosophy, sense of purpose/calling
22. **Forgiveness**: merciful, benevolent, kind
23. **Playfulness**: humour, amusing, childlike
24. **Enthusiasm**: passion, zest, infectious, engaged.

*Source*: Furnham and Lester (2012).

This would all be understandable if derailment was rare. But the statistics provide evidence otherwise. There have been 12 papers published over the last 25 years that have made good estimates of management failure. The average of these estimates is 47 percent. Yes, they are estimates, and yes, there are different definitions of failure. Suffice to say that failure extends from imprisonment (for corruption and so on) through sacking to resignation long before the employment contract ended. Management failure occurs when the person appointed to the job fails to deliver the set objectives, often with dire consequences. In short, derailment and disappointment are as common as success.

There are observable and hidden costs to all this. The share price tumbles or starts a long decline but it is the hidden costs that are greater.

They include demoralised, disengaged, less productive staff; the loss of intellectual and social capital as turnover of good people increases; and missed business opportunities.

The paradox is that most failures have previously had very successful careers. The derailed were once the high flyers. Indeed, what helped them to climb to the top also led to their demise. Yet, for many (especially those who appointed them), their failure comes as a great surprise. However, retrospectively, going through the "case history," the clues are all there. Alas, it is only hindsight that is 20/20.

One of the "lessons" from all this is to make someone responsible for selecting out CEOs. The way that most appointments are made is to look for evidence of certain attributes or competencies. Usually, *more is better:* you can't be too creative or too customer focused; it is impossible to be too analytic or have too much integrity … or even to be too "good with people." But the evidence suggests the opposite. It is called the *spectrum hypothesis* and suggests that extremes of normality are abnormality. There is no clear dividing line between normality and pathology as it is a spectrum. Thus, very high self-esteem may be seen as clinical narcissism.

It is perhaps just as important to have selectors look for evidence of characteristics that they do not want. A good list is:

- *Arrogance*: They are right and everybody else is wrong.
- *Melodrama*: They want to be the centre of attention.
- *Volatility*: Their mood swings create business swings.
- *Excessive caution*: They can't make important decisions.
- *Habitual distrust*: They focus on the negatives all the time.
- *Aloofness*: They disengage and disconnect from staff.
- *Eccentricity*: They think it is fun to be different just for the sake of it.
- *Passive resistance*: Their silence is misinterpreted as agreement.
- *Perfectionism*: They seem to get the little things right even if the big things go wrong.
- *Eagerness to please*: They stress that being popular matters most.

The evidence suggests that derailment is a function of three things: very particular personality traits; naïve followers; and particular situations that mean poorly regulated and governed businesses.

We look, first, at potentially derailing leaders. Researchers in this area now talk of the dark triad of *subclinical psychopathy*. These individuals score high on anti-social and narcissistic personality disorder while having

Machiavellian beliefs and behaviors. The three interrelated features of the dark side are:

- arrogance, self-centredness, self-enhancement;
- duplicitousness, cynicism, manipulativeness; and
- emotional coldness, impulsive thrill-seeking and frequent engagement in illegal, dangerous and anti-social behavior.

The argument is this. Dark triad traits facilitate the exploitation of others in short-term social contexts because:

- narcissists are agentic, dominant, eager for power;
- Machiavellians can be exploitative charmers; and
- psychopaths have an exploitative nature.

"People of the dark triad" are high in self-interest but low in empathy. They are therefore not interested in, well suited to, or good at, long-term relationships where a degree of reciprocity is called for. They are often found out, so prefer a "hit-and-run" strategy.

But if they are articulate, bright and educated, as well as good-looking, the behaviors associated with the dark triad probably help them to climb the greasy pole of business life. The bright ones do well in the city. The less talented individuals with the dark triad are more likely to turn out to be confidence tricksters, petty criminals and imposters.

People of the dark triad gain a reputation for boldness and self-confidence, pushing through change, cutting back dead wood. They are thought to be adventurous and often mischievous, sometimes bullies. Any names come to mind?

We look next at the types of people who allow derailing leaders to thrive. We get the politicians and leaders we deserve. It has been said that there are toxic followers. Many have attempted to categorize these into different groups such as bystanders, acolytes, true believers or, more simply, conformers and colluders. Conformers tend to be immature with a negative self-concept, while colluders are more selfish, ambitious, destructive and openly supportive of toxic tyrants.

What are they like, these toxic board members who even encourage derailing leaders? *First*, most have low self-esteem, which they hope the leader will be able to improve. They also tend to be helpless and fatalistic, expecting the leader to give them power and influence. Toxic leaders reinforce these board members' sense of passivity while giving them a hope of escape.

*Second*, toxic followers also tend to be morally immature: their sense of right and wrong is weak, and conformity to immoral behavior dictated by the leader occurs. Vulnerable, immature, impressionable adults make good followers of strong but destructive leaders. Under-socialized or morally undeveloped people are happy to endorse the violence of toxic leaders.

*Third*, toxic followers yearn for rank, status and power: people ambitious for status and land/*Lebensraum* make better followers. The more they see that there is psychological and material profit to be gained by following, the more quickly and happily they follow.

*Fourth*, they share the values and beliefs of their leaders, who are often fundamentalists and based on some in-group superiority. Simply, followers who share world views with those of the destructive leader are naturally more likely to follow them.

But the social, economic and legal climate can help or hinder the dark-triad leader. They do best in situations of flux and instability. Political, economic and social instability are very frightening. Toxic leaders exploit fluidity, advocating radical means of restoring peace, harmony and progress. They are granted excessive authority and power that they are reluctant to relinquish. Next, the more people feel personally threatened, the more internal and external enemies they see around them, and the happier they are to follow toxic leaders who promise them security. Third, dark-triad leaders do best in cultures that are uncomfortable around ambiguity and uncertainty; those that have elaborate rules and rituals offering easy solutions to complex problems are easier to control. Further, the more there is a disparity between rich and poor, educated and uneducated, high and low status, the more the toxic leader thrives.

But the most important factor is where corporate governance is weak: where power is centralized and those monitoring authority and responsibility are silenced. This is like removing the internal audit from the organization. It means the end of constraint and monitoring.

The issue is always an appropriate balance between over- versus under-regulation. There is a cost to supplying the information required for good corporate governance. It may be that paying too much attention to internal auditing and the supply of accounting information taxes the organization too heavily.

Some leaders feel quite rightly that they are handicapped, even trapped, by the requirements of corporate governance. They feel they cannot act quickly or boldly enough to do what has to be done. They see governance not as a wise system of checks and balances but as a suffocating system of bureaucracy that leads to long-term failure.

Often business and political leaders have significant decisional and behavioral latitude. But can this discretion, this latitude, be a significant derailer? Discretion is freedom, freedom is power, and power can corrupt. Some senior jobs involve a great deal of responsibility but not much discretion. Rules and regulations, ever-watchful shareholders and the media, in addition to financial and other constraints, simply reduce the opportunities of the grown-ups to misbehave, make mistakes or simply to "lose the plot."

Good managers are characterized by various phenomena. Often they tend pro-actively to seek feedback from trusted, honest observers throughout their career to monitor how they are doing. Next, they seek out opportunities to grow, develop, learn or upgrade important skills. They also seek a formal or informal coach or mentor to help them through times of acute change or transition. In short, they seek out sources of assessment, challenge and support.

Those prone to derailment do not do this. Through hubris, anxiety or lack of insight, they have to be given "developmental" assignments and coerced to go on. They might go on short, taught, leadership programs, but few later cite such events as crucial ingredients in their development. They need opportunities to examine their style, strengths and weaknesses with intensive and honest feedback. Paradoxically, perhaps an early career failure or mishap can be an excellent learning experience to ensure that mistakes are not repeated.

Coaching for executives can help a great deal. Some organizations have prescribed mentoring where every manager at a certain level is mentored by a person above him or her.

Despite putting in place such support, not all derailment can be prevented. However, much can be done to help the stressed leader who is crossing the thin line between poor management and pathology.

The cost of derailment is high for the individual manager and his/her family, peers and subordinates, and for the company as a whole. Often derailment is quite unexpected. Yet nearly always a more careful and critical review of derailed leaders' biographies contain all the cues that derailment might occur. By then it is too late.

Organizations can reduce, rather than prevent or eliminate, the prospect of their senior leaders and managers derailing, by ensuring good governance and strong management processes. Leaders need enough free-dom to manoeuvre but not unlimited power.

All leaders work with "top teams" called boards, cabinets or some-thing of the sort. These groups can easily become highly dysfunctional and themselves be a cause of management derailment. It is desirable to have someone monitor the health of boards from time to time.

There are many stages when derailment may be addressed. The most obvious are recruitment and selection. There is now much more interest in this issue, and excellent psychometrically validated tests to evaluate the dark side of personality. These can indicate possible areas of concern about the behavior of leaders when put under pressure, which they inevi-tably are.

Coaching and mentoring can help. Paradoxically, those who need it the most also resist it most and benefit from it least. It takes a highly skilled coach to confront a very senior manager/leader and help him/her to avoid derailment.

A simple selection model is shown in Figure I.2. Everyone is con-cerned with getting A but nobody wants D. The question is: 'Who does the selecting out: What do they look for?'

## Conclusion

It is alas true that we are not all talented. Talent to succeed at work, like everything else, is normally distributed in a bell curve. It is sad to see

|  | Good | Bad |
|---|---|---|
| Select | A | B |
| Reject | C | D |

*Figure I.2*   A simple selection model

talent not explored and wasted, and tragic to see the less talented stumble and fall in the workplace.

There are certain "course requirements" to be included within the talent/potential group. But they are necessary and not sufficient. Experience and education bring out talent.

## References

Athey, R. (2008) *Do You Know Where Your talent Is?* London: Deloitte Development.

Berger, L. (2004) "Creating a Talent Management System for Organisation Excellence," in L. Berger and D. Berger, *The Talent Management Handbook.* New York: McGraw-Hill, 3–21.

Berger, L. and Berger, D. (2004) *The Talent Management Handbook.* New York: McGraw Hill.

Brody, L. (2005) "The Study of Exceptional Talent," *High Ability Studies, 16,* 87–96.

Brody, L. and Mills, C. (2005) "Talent Search Research," *High Ability Studies, 16,* 97–111.

Clarke, B. (1988) *Growing Up Gifted.* Columbus, OH: Charles E. Merrill.

Corporate Leadership Council (2001) *Voice of the Leader: A Quantitative Analysis of Leadership Bench Strength and Development Strategies.* Washington, DC: Corporate Excutive Board.

Cox, C. and Cooper, C. (1988) *High Flyers: An Anatomy of Managerial Success.* Oxford: Basil Blackwell.

Economist Intelligence Unit (2006) *The CEO's Role in Talent Management.* London: EIU.

Furnham, A. (2003) "The Icarus Syndrome: Talent Management and Derailment in the New Millennium," in M. Effron, R. Gandossy and M. Goldsmith (eds), *Human Resources in the 21st Century.* New York: Wiley, pp. 99–108.

Furnham, A. (2007) "Personality Disorders and Derailment at Work: The Paradoxical Positive Influence of Pathology in the Workplace," in J. Langen-Fox, C. Cooper and R. Klimoski (eds), *Management Challenges and Symptoms of the Dysfunctional Workplace.* Cheltenham: Edward Elgar.

Furnham, A. and Lester, D. (2012) "Development of a Short Measure of Character Strength," *European Journal of Psychological Assessment.*

Gagne, F. (2004) "Transforming gifts into talents," *High Ability Studies, 15,* 119–47.

Gladwell, M. (2002) "The Talent Myth," *The New Yorker,* 22 July, 28–33.

Gunter, B. and Furnham, A. (2001) *Assessing Business Potential.* London: Whurr.

Harvey, J. and Katz, C. (1985) *If I'm So Successful, Why Do I Feel Like a Fake? The Imposter Phenomenon.* New York: St. Martin's Press.

Heller, K., Monks, F. and Passow, A. (eds) (1993) *International Handbook of Research and Development of Giftedness and Talent.* New York: Pergamon Press.

Jennings, R., Cox, C. and Cooper, C. (1994) *Business Elites: The Psychology of Entrepreneurs.* London: Routledge.

Locke, E. (1997) "Prime Movers. The Traits of Great Business Leaders," in C. Cooper and S. Jackson (eds), *Creating Tomorrow's Organisations.* Chichester: Wiley, pp. 75–96.

Martin, J. and Schmidt, C. (2010) 'How to Keep Your Top Talented," *Harvard Business Review*, May, 54–61.

McCall, M. (1994) "Identifying Leadership Potential in Future International Executives," *Consulting Psychology Journal, 46*, 49–63.

McCall, M. (1998) *High Flyers: Developing the Next Generation of Leaders*. Boston, MA: Harvard Business Press.

McCall, M., Lombardo, M. and Morrison, A. (1990) *The Lessons of Experience: How Successful Executives Develop on the Job*. Lexington, MA: Lexington Books.

McCall, M., Spreitzer, G. and Mahoney, J. (1995) "Identifying Leadership Potential in Future International Executives," in D. Ready (ed.), *In Charge of Change: Insights into Next-generation Organizations* (Lexington, MA: International Consortium for Executive Development Research).

Michaels, E., Handfield-Jones, H. and Axelrod, B. (2001) *The War for Talent*. Boston, MA: Harvard Business School Press.

Paulus, D. and Williams, K. (2002) "The Dark Triad of Personality," *Journal of Research in Personality, 36*, 556–63.

Robinson, C., Fetters, R., Riester, D., and Bracco, A. (2009) "The Paradox of Potential," *Industrial and Organizational Psychology, 2*, 413–15.

Silzer, R. and Church, A. (2009) "The Pearls and Perils of Identifying Potential," *Industrial and Organisational Psychology, 2*, 377–412.

Shavinina, L. (2004) "Explaining High Abilities of Nobel Laureates," *High Ability Studies, 15*, 243–54.

Spreitzer, G., McCall, M. and Mahoney, R. (1997) "Early Identification of International Executive Potential," *Journal of Applied Psychology, 82*, 6–29.

Vijver, F. van de (2008) "Personality Assessment of Global Talent: Conceptual and Methodological Issues," *International Journal of Testing, 8*, 304–14.

# A walk in the woods

In the old days, when (usually male) interviewers were selecting (usually male) applicants for a senior position they were taken to lunch. This was especially the case if the applicant had been to a good school and college (Oxbridge), belonged to a good club and had the experience the interviewer required.

Lunch could be a pretty protracted affair and certainly involved a good claret – chosen by the interviewee, paid for by the interviewer. Indeed, that was one of the small but significant tests. It was also an excellent environment in which to have a really good natter. Subtle things can be approached subtly. There are interruptions, pauses, and "bathroom breaks" to contemplate and regroup as well as empty the bladder.

Meals are symbolic in all cultures. They celebrate companionship, friendship and festivity. Wine can loosen tongues and bring about good cheer. They test many skills.

Conversations in trains and taxis, airport lounges and airplanes can be very illuminating: the "bare-all" conversations between complete strangers at 30,000 feet fuelled by wine, boredom and fatigue. Fellow passengers become confessors and counselors. And there is nothing like the shared misery of flight delay, a train breakdown or a slow-moving queue to initiate a good chinwag.

The question of "where" has not escaped those whose discipline is the study of place. In a recent issue of *Applied Geography,* Evans and Jones (2011) discuss the "walking interview." There is, believe it or not, already a literature on the subject. The argument is that walking interviews generate "richer" data because interviewees are more honest in these circumstances, and are prompted by meanings and connections in their surroundings.

The fundamental questions of this odd academic bywater are: what is the relationship between what people say and where they say it; and what is the qualitative and quantitative difference between the data generated by walking and sedentary interviews? And the answers? Well, people talk more about place (landscape, buildings and environment) when walking, and they tend to "go on a bit."

Indeed, is there not a (somewhat obscure) television programme where the host (a comic of sorts) interviews his (a little past their sell-by-date) celebrity guests in a car as he drives? Perhaps it would be better if the guest drove? And where is health-and-safety in all this? Why not a Dutch-type cycle-ride interview? True, it would be discriminatory – the old, the infirm and the disabled couldn't take part.

So we use sedentary versus mobile interview methods. Get the gist: sedentary is lazy, dull, old-fashioned; mobile is for people on the move, aspirational, pushing forward.

There are a few questions to be asked if you are planning a walking interview. *First*, who plans the route: interviewer or interviewee? *Second*, how carefully is it planned: a meandering ramble or a sort of guided walking tour? *Third*, should it be urban or rural? *Fourth*, how arduous should it be: heart-racing or quiet strolling?

If the interviewee chooses the route, could we consider this a test – what psychologists call a *projective technique*? Imagine the following: your potential employer has asked you to arrange a two-hour walking interview in the South-East. You are given the time slot and told to let the interviewers know where they are to meet. So what would you do? A brisk circumambulation of Hyde Park; a stroll along the South Bank of the river; a complex criss-crossing of the Docklands? Should the route be meticulously planned and Sat-Nav guided, or should you bumble about as the spirit moves?

What does your route say about you? Is the detailed map planner an obsessional control freak? Does a three-mile hike show a person's ambition, determination and fitness? Should you ask the interviewees their thought processes about the task when the interview is over? And will they be so distracted by following the route they can't answer questions clearly?

There are other ideas to enrich the standard office-based interview, where both parties are on their best behavior, skilfully concealing their real selves behind a smokescreen of clever impression management. One option is to ask the interviewee to bring to the interview some object that really helps the interviewer understand them. So keen rugby players might bring a ball, or golfers a club. But what would you think of someone who brought a copy of the Koran or a bottle of whisky? Surely this would just test the artfulness of interviewees and their skill at assimilation. Bring a laptop showing you like to work on the journey to work (conscientiousness); your certificate of a parachute jump (tough, courageous); a photograph of the starving African children whom you sponsor (agreeableness); your best painting (creativity). Best leave your Blue Peter badge and Scout uniform at home.

Certainly it's time to rethink and reenergize the standard job interview in the office. If the task is to get to know the real person, the issue must be to find a way to get the type of information you need.

The trouble with the dining, walk or special-object approach is that it rewards only one type of individual. But worse, each can be highly misleading or often down-right wrong: amateur psychologizing may seriously misinterpret or overinterpret the interviewee's behavior, personality and motives. But given the importance of selection, there must be ways of conducting better interviews.

## Reference

Evans, J. and Jones, P. (2011) "The Walking Interview: Methodology, Mobility and Place," *Applied Geography*, 31: 849–58.

# Aberrant self-promotion at work

Work psychologists have identified an increasingly common syndrome in the workplace: aberrant self-promotion (ASP). The pattern was identified nearly 20 years ago, and those with this style seem to be increasingly noticeable.

Those who first described it talked of "the dark side of normal" and "subclinical pathology." They argued that mental illness should not be seen as categorical: "you are or you are not a …" psychopath, neurotic, schizophrenic, but rather mental illness is just an extreme dimension of normality. Just as some people are extremely tall or fat or strong – they are abnormal. Thus the extreme introvert can appear to be pathologically shy and uncommunicative.

Further, people with all sorts of (even severe) mental illnesses can survive, and even thrive, in society. The anxiety- and depression-prone neurotic can function perfectly adequately in society, given the right conditions.

The whole "care in the community" message was that those who are mentally ill can function in open society to the benefit of all. Sceptics saw this as a cynical cost-cutting move to close down mental hospitals and throw the inmates into the less-than-warm embrace and enthusiasm of local groups.

While the message has got through that mental illness is very common, nothing to be ashamed of, and not necessarily a serious social or occupational handicap, another idea has been growing. That is, that some manifestations of mental illness may actually be beneficial to certain activities and careers. Most people will recognize this idea when they think about creativity. The link between creativity and bipolar disorder, schizophrenia and hypermania has been established. Creatives have, quite rightly, a reputation for being odd, difficult and unconventional.

The idea of a subclinical condition is that it is not severe enough to be considered as a serious mental illness or require treatment. So the obsessive-compulsive can thrive in quality control; the paranoid in the security business, and those with a strong hint of hysterical personality disorder can thrive in the entertainment world.

Which brings us back to the aberrant self-promoter. Those who show the characteristics of the syndrome are said to be exploitative, dominating and grandiose, superficial and manipulative, and consider themselves entitled. They also show little guilt or remorse for their selfishness and generally show little empathy for the condition of others.

Psychometricians have devised tests to measure ASP. Here are some of the statements that ASP individuals characteristically make or endorse: "My ideas are nearly always better than other people's"; "Sometimes rules don't apply to me"; "I like to live on the edge."

Clinicians see ASP as a heady mixture of subclinical narcissism, impulsivity and anti-social personality disorder. It's about the selfish, callous and remorseless exploitation of other people while at the same time demanding respect and admiration.

Early studies of students who manifest this behavior pattern showed they admitted to cheating, lying and other manipulative behavior to change their grades as well as having more parking tickets, police arrests and judicial reprimands.

A study by Wu and Lebreton (2011) looked at these people at work. The assumption was that ASP was closely linked to a whole range of counterproductive behaviors. The study examined three broad areas: accidents, safety orientation and the infringement of safety rules.

The ASP person enjoys defying authority. They are thrill-seeking and reckless. They break, disregard and challenge rules. Logically, then, they are more likely to be involved in accidents, both big and small. They set a bad example to others. They are the bane of Health and Safety officers, of course. And, as always, there are costs involved.

Next, absenteeism. People in Britain have an average of eight days' absence from work per year: twice as many in the public sector compared to the private sector. It is difficult to estimate the cost, though it has been estimated to be between £200 and £2,000 per day.

Conscientious people feel a duty to their employers, coworkers and customers. They struggle in to work even if they don't feel well, if they are unhappy or have some personal problem. But not the "me, me, me" – focused ASP person: offered a better option somewhere else, they are happy to abandon their work.

And then there is job turnover: voluntary or not. Again, a serious cost to the employer as new staff have to be recruited, selected and trained. It's not difficult to see why ASP people are more likely to be sacked. And why they are more prone to believing the grass is greener elsewhere. Job histories always tell a story. If, of course, you are told the truth.

So what of the demography of ASP employees? Are they more likely to be male or female; young or old; in the service or manufacturing sector?

The data are not in for population samples, but there do seem to be slightly more ASP males than females and younger versus older people.

ASP employees are particularly problematic if they are bright, good-looking and articulate. All these factors help their manipulative streak and feed their self-obsession. They are then able to exploit everyone so much more easily to the cost of all.

## Reference

Wu, J. and Lebreton, J. (2011) "Reconsidering the Dispositional Basis of Counterproductive Work Behaviour: The Role of Aberrant Personality," *Personnel Psychology*, 64: 593–626.

# All the questions and all the answers

Fanatics and moderates exist as much in business as in religion and politics. By definition, fanatics are extremists: some may be violent; many militant; all authoritarian. They have a distinctive mentality or mind set. And it is one with clear answers, an agenda and always a righteous cause.

Since the Second World War, psychologists have studied a wide array of extremist groups: Anarchists, Bolsheviks, Fascists, Nazis and more recently Islamist militant extremists. One analysis (Moghaddam, 2005) identified a dozen or so features of the mind set of those with all the answers:

1. Perceived personal and group deprivation in relation to others.
2. A broad, pervasive dissatisfaction with the world as it is.
3. A refusal to model themselves on some externally imposed idea (the modern Western liberal) of how one should behave.
4. A sense of being constantly and historically unfairly treated by powerful others, with a consequent abiding feeling of injustice.
5. The feeling that no one has a real say in important decisions, leading to a feeling of helplessness.
6. An aggressive attitude and stance toward a very particular and identifiable enemy who is/was the real source of all their problems.
7. The simple sense of the end justifying the means in order to obtain justice and restitution for oneself and one's group.
8. A clear us-versus-them, black/white, kill or be killed style of thinking.
9. A strong belief that their cause is all that they are living for.
10. An obligation to follow all the rules and conform to the behavioral norms of the group.
11. A conviction that "heroic acts" will improve the world as a whole.
12. A utopian vision of a different, better world.

Researchers in America, Central Europe and Singapore (Saurcier et al., 2011) have identified various themes in the mind set of militant extremists. A useful checklist to detect possible terrorists at work? A way of predicting whether someone might prove to be a difficult trade unionist?

The *first* is that difficult situations necessitate extreme, unconventional and unorthodox measures. Read: illegality, violence, brutality is OK, even desirable. The *second* is that clever trick of guilt-absolving, responsibility-denying gobbledegook that makes their actions somehow morally defensible. *Third*, a lot of military terminology and discourse: look for reference to army, battlefield, armed, struggle and war. All the imagery, metaphors and even the pace of talk are clearly militaristic. *Fourth*, the clear belief that one's group is being tragically and unjustly obstructed and denied its rightful position in the world. A downtrodden, neglected and despised group ... who are, of course, the chosen ones.

*Fifth*, there is a simple, inaccurate view of history where in the past there was a glorious, golden age: a period when they were "top dog," the superior culture, and they are inheritors of that magnificent tradition. This was usually a very long time ago and full of myth and legend with very little real historical data. *Sixth*, and related to the above, delusional utopanizing: a clear belief in the possibility of a new civilization, a harmonious, ever-lasting paradise.

*Seventh*, an obsession with calamity, catastrophe and crisis: a way of portraying the present in very alarmist terms. *Eighth*, and probably more associated with religious militants, the idea of "deus ex machina;" interventions of miracles and supernatural interventions of hope from above. *Ninth*, in this tradition, the imperative to rid the world of evil; to purify the land and people so that they are cleansed of corruption, the stain of the infidel, the mark of Cain.

*Tenth*, and perhaps the most worrying, the glorification of martyrdom: of dying for the cause and being a just sacrifice for the glory of the cause. This is pure *kamikaze*.

*Eleventh*, that all good people have a duty and obligation to follow the dictates of the cause, namely both to defend and to attack; there is a sense of pressure at work here – no choice, no ifs-and-buts. *Twelfth*, that old stalwart Machiavellianism in the service of the cause: immoral means to immortal ends, force to achieve the goal.

*Thirteenth*, a curious desire to turn acceptable behaviors and beliefs such as bellicosity, intolerance and vengeance into virtues. Children of an angry God despise cowardice, moderation and forgiveness. It is the world turned upside down.

*Fourteenth*, a not uncommon trait of dehumanizing, demonizing and denouncing opponents as animals, devils or *Untermenschlich*: sub-human.

The final two beliefs are shared by many. One is the idea that the modern world, indeed all aspects of modernity, are disastrous for humanity – selfish, sinful, materialistic, wasteful. But there is the more worrying view that the democratically elected civil government is actually illegitimate. The rulers, authorities and the elected have overstepped acceptable moral bounds and essentially forfeited their right to govern.

But is this militant-extremist fanatical thinking pattern utterly bizarre and essentially representing the beliefs of mad people? Not at all: some extreme environmentalists, animal rights activists and politicians hold such views. Believe you belong to a superior, vulnerable and helpless group that is unjustly treated – or that you speak on their behalf – and you have it in a nutshell.

## References

Moghaddam, F. (2005) "The Staircase to Terrorism: A Psychological Exploration," *American Psychologist*, 60: 161–5.

Saurcier, G., Akers, L., Shen-Miller, S., Knezevie, G.M. and Stankov, L. (2011) "Patterns of Thinking in Militant Extremism," *Perspectives on Psychological Science*, 4: 256–71.

# Appraisal systems

A little quiz…

| | | Agree/Disagree | | | |
|---|---|---|---|---|---|
| 1. | I have found my appraisals always to be helpful in guiding my own career development progress. | 5 4 3 2 1 |
| 2. | The appraisal system we have is of little use to me in my efforts toward developing my subordinates' capabilities. | 5 4 3 2 1 |
| 3. | Our performance appraisal system often leaves me more uncertain about where I stand after my appraisal than before. | 5 4 3 2 1 |
| 4. | The appraisal system we use is helpful to communicate clearly to my subordinates exactly where they stand. | 5 4 3 2 1 |
| 5. | When management makes major decisions about management positions and promotions, they have access to, and make use of, performance appraisal records. | 5 4 3 2 1 |
| 6. | In making pay, promotion, transfer and other administrative personnel decisions, I am not able to obtain past performance appraisal records that could help me to make good decisions. | 5 4 3 2 1 |
| 7. | The appraisal system requires lazy or incompetent managers to do their job properly. | 5 4 3 2 1 |
| 8. | It might not be perfect but there are few serious working alternatives to our appraisal system. | 5 4 3 2 1 |
| 9. | Our appraisal system is a pointless, worthless HR bureaucratic, time-wasting exercise. | 5 4 3 2 1 |
| 10. | I look forward to my appraisals. | 5 4 3 2 1 |

In 1957, Douglas McGregor wrote an article in the *Harvard Business Review* that was rather sceptical of appraisal systems. In it, he argued that they had three basic aims: to provide data to make better "people" decisions (salary, promotion, success, transfer); to let employees know how they were doing (and what to do differently); and to be a means of coaching and development.

But most appraisal systems fail badly. Ask any audience of 100 working adults: are they happy or satisfied with their appraisal system? You'd be lucky to find half a dozen who would say yes, and they would all be from HR. Appraisal systems give HR a bad name. But why? Surely the aims make good sense. You must be able to make better people decisions with better data, and surely people need clear feedback on how they are (or should be) performing, and it can't be a bad idea to help people find and develop their strengths. True, but is the appraisal system working for or against these aims.

Systems fail for obvious and logical reasons. These have been documented many times:

1. *Managers are not trained in how to use the system.* How to set objectives or specify success criteria. How to conduct a meaningful appraisal session so that there is real dialogue, no hidden agendas and sensitive, differentiating scoring.
2. *Staff development plays little part in a manager's own appraisal.* Are managers devoted to, and rewarded for, actually developing their staff? Do they believe in coaching, training and mentoring, or not? And do they know how to fulfill these roles?
3. *Staff are passive observers, not active participants in the whole process.* Are the appraisees active or passive participants in the appraisal process? Do they believe appraisal is something done to them, for them or by them? Do appraisees have a role in setting their own goals and standards and monitoring their performance?
4. *Appraisals are full of accusations, denials and excuses, not about how to work well.* Are appraisal sessions forward-looking, focused on problem-solving, or are they strictly evaluative in looking only at past performance? Are they blame-storming sessions or attempts to improve future performance? In other words, is the appraiser a judge or a counselor or in some way simultaneously both?
5. *The effort involved in the process is not proportionate to the rewards.* Does the effort – what we still call "paperwork" in the "paperless office" – place an unreasonable workload or burden on managers? Is it all really demonstrably a good investment of time? Are managers, particularly those who manage more than a dozen subordinates, given any help or support?
6. *Appraisal data is stored but rarely used.* Is all the information gathered in this process accessible and useful in decision-making? If not, what is the point of the whole exercise?
7. *The system is too generic and vague.* Are the appraisals tailored enough to the needs of the individual workers? Or, if they are, have they become so idiosyncratic individuals cannot be compared?
8. *The appraisal system is confused with the pay for performance system.* And when profits are low and bonuses small, it seems a pointless paperchase.

9.  *Managers are punished for not doing any, or any good, appraisals, but never rewarded for doing them well.* Should conducting appraisals be part of the central job description of managers?
10. *Appraisals are increasing a legal necessity.* It becomes very problematic, if not impossible, to dismiss an incompetent, lazy or feckless employee without an appraisal.

There are different takes on the whole appraisal process. The opinions of the giver and of the receiver are at variance. It is strange how most want to receive but few want to give. There is also the HR perspective, with the shadow of the Finance Department in the background.

But increasingly there is a legal perspective on performance appraisal. That always seems to focus the mind more clearly than all the memos sent down from Personnel.

# Beware of creatives

There is a creativity industry as active, proselytizing and confident as the stress industry. The latter wants to persuade us that nearly everyone is stressed (at work). Work stress is almost exclusively the fault of employers; you need to be compensated for it; and there are many (expensive) courses you can attend that will help. It is in the best interests, of course, of this industry to exaggerate the incidence and consequences of stress to keep their business going.

The creative industry has similar mantras. The first is that, as the stress counselors suggest about work stress, we are all creative; or at least potentially creative. Once we are liberated, set free, set on fire, unblocked … or something similar, we can all discover our inner child, our latent Michelangelo or whatever. But, of course, you need to buy a book, hear a lecture or attend a course to work out how to do it.

The second axiom is that all of us, everywhere, need creative individuals to thrive and survive. Not only in the creative industries of advertising and theatre, but absolutely everywhere – in the local council housing department; in the supermarket warehouse; and on your holiday jet.

But there can be a slur attached to some aspects of the word "creative." "Creative" accountancy appears to blur the line between avoidance and evasion. Getting "creative" with the revenue generation stream could mean acting in an underhand way to maximize profits.

What the creative industry peddles is a positive view of creativity both as fun and as crucially important. It holds up wholesome examples of people who are seen as the epitome of creativity: wonderfully talented, often demure geniuses who have been the savior of mankind.

The psychological literature on creative types tells a rather different story. Certainly creatives – at least in the arts – have a vivid imagination, a life of the mind, and curiosity. They are divergent thinkers with quirky ideas: many impractical, almost magical ideas can flow out of them.

But what about creativity and personality? There is no clear relationship between introversion–extraversion and creativity. Some creatives are sociable partygoers; others are inhibited and introverted recluses. Artists and writers? More likely the latter. Musicians? More likely the former: the very nature of their work is in groups.

And what about neuroticism, social adjustment or whatever? Are creatives more likely to be worriers, socially anxious, prone to depression or hypochondriacal? Again, it takes all sorts. There is a worrying, but fortunately weak, link between creativity and suicide, and there have been some very well-known cases (Alexander McQueen, the dress designer, being a recent example).

The two clear and consistent attributes closely associated with those known to be highly creative are tough-mindedness and unreliability. Creatives tend to be low on the personality trait of both agreeableness and conscientiousness.

Agreeable people are kind and forgiving; empathic and warm; trusting and generous. Creativity test scores are nearly always strongly *negatively* correlated with agreeableness. Creatives are selfish and tough-minded; egocentric and rude; abrupt and even cruel. They speak their mind, whatever the consequences. In short, they are rather disagreeable. Not easy to work with and not much fun to be around.

But, worse, they often have a very low score on the work ethic. They don't pitch up and pitch in as others do. They are unreliable, frequently disorganized and disrespectful of those in authority. You can't depend on them doing what they have agreed or promised. They may well be creative geniuses, but getting them to deliver on time as specified is a near impossibility.

Unfortunately, some are touched by an even more dangerous affliction: *narcissistic personality disorder.* These consider themselves to be the entitled, who need admiration, respect and obedience from everybody around them, all the time. Their needs must be paramount, fulfilled completely and immediately.

Criticism at any time by anyone is to be outlawed and punished. In their eyes they are super-gifted, unique, and deserve all the recognition they get.

So the psychometric literature paints a less flattering picture of creativity: not very likeable, difficult to work with and egocentric individuals. Yes, of course, there are exceptions, but this is what the data says, at least for creativity in the arts. However, the picture is somewhat different in the sciences.

But is creativity not essential to business survival? We need not only to adapt and change, but also lead the way. Creatives lead, others follow. Creatives find the breakthrough, spot gaps, but most of all come up with new inventions.

There is, however, all the difference in the world between *creatives* and *innovators*. One has the idea; the other puts it into practice. One produces the blueprint; the other takes it to market. One sits in the attic, the shed or the studio; the other in the boardroom, seminar room or sales office.

So does your company need dozens of really creative people? Probably not. Are you willing to put up with the serious consequences of trying to manage a whole kaleidoscope of creatives? Unwise.

The best policy, then, is to hire creative consultants on an occasional basis, and employ innovators. Equally important, hire those who can spot creative ideas. Buy patents, and buy the product, but not the producer.

# Blamestorming

The political correctness police get everywhere. They have recently outlawed the term "brainstorming," invented by an American advertising executive over 50 years ago. It is thought to insult, upset and demean those who have seizures. So now we have "thought-showering sessions."

This news has not affected the Europeans: the French, Germans and Italians still offer invitations to "le/der/il brainstorming sessions". Ask anyone from anywhere what brainstorming is in their language and they are stumped: like Bulgarian wine, it doesn't travel.

Years ago, wags invented the concept of "blamestorming". This is where a group of people get together to attribute blame after a (usually serious) cock-up. They might pretend the meeting is to learn the lessons that caused the problem, but no, it's really to unload guilt and find a scapegoat or culprit.

Journalists, too, have got in on the act, as have ambulance-chasing lawyers. They don't ask for neutral attributions – "Who or what caused the accident?" But rather "Whom do you blame for the accident?"

Psychologists have long been interested in the attributions of cause. They talk of errors. The *fundamental* attribution error is to explain your behavior in terms of contextual and situational pressures and constraints, but others' behavior in terms of personality. I failed because of my teacher; they failed because they were dim.

Then there is the *ultimate* attribution error. This is the tendency to explain your and your group's success (promotion, wage increase, productivity) as a result of effort and ability, but your failures as a result of fate, chance or situational factors. Further, the opposite is the case for your enemies: they succeed through corruption and fail because they are not very able.

Politicians play this game superbly. Do you remember the Iron Chancellor (Gordon Brown) saying, when times were good, that his policies had "abolished boom and bust," then that the collapsing economy was all a result of macroeconomic forces quite beyond his control.

Clinical psychologists have also noted this behavior pattern. An American psychologist in the 1930s claimed there were three classic behavior patterns displayed when individuals were faced with anger and frustration, disappointment and failure. These were:

- *Extrapunitiveness*: the habit, tendency or preference to unfairly, unreasonably (but skilfully) blame others.
- *Impunitiveness*: this is to simply deny your role in the failure or to challenge whether the failure was really one at all.
- *Intropunitiveness*: this is the tendency both to exaggerate failure and to blame yourself too harshly, with excessive guilt.

Note that all three are considered types of defence mechanisms. All are ways of dealing with failure. They are *psycho*logical rather than logical reactions, which may be thought of as an attempt to examine critically the manifold causes of the behavior.

There are three fundamental questions regarding blamestorming. The *first* and perhaps most important is what sorts of individuals choose to use the strategy. We know that people are pretty consistent in their patterns.

Some blame those who assign, rather than carry out the task. Some expect failure and therefore in a self-fulfilling way actually encourage it. Extrapunitive (blame-others) types develop sophisticated theories and language to hand out the blame for anything they might be part of. Impunitiveness is also quite common. They might distort information to avoid blame, or attempt to ingratiate themselves with others. Some seem not to care much about failure, or to reframe it. Some expect immediate, total and unmitigated forgiveness for everything, while others prefer complex, near fatalistic explanations for these problems.

The intropunitive accept blame but too readily and too much. They criticize themselves for small errors and shoulder the blame excessively. They must be distinguished from those who accept blame as an attention-seeking device, preferring that to being ignored.

The *second* issue is the psychological health of these three defences. It's not difficult to see the current cultural answer: there seems to be a psychobabbly, cultural endorsement of extrapunitiveness. It's healthy to place the blame elsewhere. It's good for you. All part wrapped up in the narcissist-developing, entitlement mind sets that are found among young people.

Clearly, excessive self-blame leads to martyr-like depression. It's not good to take on the sins of the whole world; to let people off the hook; or to be excessively self-critical. That is the road to depression, passivity and lack of achievement.

Impunitiveness is also not much help. Lessons can be learned from failure, but burying your head in the sand or rebranding your mistakes doesn't work.

So, *third*, what advice to give people faced with failure? Have a good look at your preferred habitual style, then try a better analysis of the cause of the failure before acting. Treat it as an inquiry to learn lessons for the future.

The quick fix of extrapunitiveness is very unhelpful at work. Being unfairly blamed can seriously alienate people and cause further failure. Denial is a river in Egypt. That doesn't work. And being a shock absorber for everything leads to helplessness.

So join the blamestorming session with your eyes open to the three types of blaming behavior. Recognize who habitually use which style. And know the consequences of adopting one style over the others.

# Career success

What do the data say about predictors of an individual's career and financial success? Demographers, economists, psychologists and sociologists have found some pretty interesting patterns.

*First*, economists have found that education level, schools and universities attended, and the kind of degree you get are strong predictors of success as measured by income. That is why parents worry so much about schools and the domino effect of starting at the "right" school. Bright, hard-working, ambitious people do well in education and figure out how the game works. Education shows people how to gain access to, and critique, information. It increases verbal, numerical and financial literacy. But it does more than that: it provides not only a good benchmark for your abilities, but also the opportunity to make important friends for life.

All education is much more about socialization than exam preparation. Good institutions offer more of everything (facilities, teaching, peers, role models) at a higher standard. They turn out more "rounded" people.

*Second*, sociologists have shown that parental social class is a strong predictor of job success. Families pass on not only genes but also social environments, "facilities" and opportunities. Middle-class parents hold values such as prudence, thrift and postponement of gratification, all of which are important in career success. People in higher social classes provide more stable and enriched environments where learning and achievement are encouraged. By definition, class is related to wealth, and therefore also to early access to the many factors that influence the development of young people.

*Third,* psychologists found that biological, biographical, intellectual and personality values are important predictors of success in the workplace. Bright, curious, open-minded people embrace change better. They spot opportunities, analyze trends and put together persuasive arguments.

Psychologists have identified various personality traits that predict quite well business, career and education success. The first is *emotional stability* or adjustment. Its opposite is neuroticism, moodiness or instability. Emotional conflicts and proneness to anxiety, stress and worry sap energy. This both serves to dilute career focus and leads to poor decision-making. There are a multitude of knocks, disappointments and setbacks on the way up the corporate ladder. How you deal with each one has an impact on the height and angle of the ladder you climb. Low-adjusted people are often flooded with anxiety, which affects their decision-making. They also are more prone to a range of illnesses, which means that the fit, in every sense of the word, speed ahead.

Next, there is that powerful grouping of factors we used to call the work ethic. These are motives or traits in people that are manifest as competitive, hard-working and focused. It is about being driven and organized, but most of all self-disciplined, and self-discipline starts early. It's more than a habit trained in people. It is about pitching up and pitching in. It's about *carpe diem*. It's about taking on responsibility. And it's very good for the reputation.

Extreme forms of conscientiousness are linked with risk aversion, which can be a problem in business. It is also undesirable when, in effect, it is compensation for being smart enough. Some second-raters have to work very hard to catch up. So it's the bright, self-disciplined person you are seeking. And there is nothing wrong with being ambitious and with a strong need for achievement.

It doesn't harm one to be creative, but it is not a course requirement, though there comes a time when one needs to learn to be strategic rather than tactical. But, paradoxically, being a warm, empathic, kind and agreeable person may not help at all. One also needs to be tough; some would even say ruthless.

Apart from choosing our parents well there is not much the young adult can do about their early environment and personality. But there is skill acquisition. There are two different but related sorts of skills you need to acquire to do well in business. The *first* are socio-emotional skills. There are many words for this: interpersonal skills, emotional intelligence, charm. Sure, some people through their personality (extraversion, agreeableness) have probably acquired more skills than others by early adulthood. But these skills can be taught and improved. It's the people skills stuff, so important in business. It's about getting along with people.

The *second* skill set is more about getting *ahead* of people. It's about political skills. More negotiation than influence. More shrewdness than Machiavellianism. The politically astute know all about the importance of reputation management. Reputation drives appraisals and references. It drives votes and the belief that one is talented. Note how carefully politicians try to guard, cherish and enhance their reputations. It is not something to be careless about.

Career success is all about striving for the control of resources, for power and for status. The evolutionary psychologists say it's a proxy for reproductive success. Some are more able to attract support and attain power.

So, if the social scientists are right, your background, ability and personality *do* matter. It helps to be born into the "right tribe," but ability and drive can and do overcome adversity. Indeed, it actually makes people more determined and hardy as their climb is all the steeper.

# The catch-phrase technique

Full English or fruit platter? Bonds or shares? Jogging or cycling? Film or theatre? No interview now seems complete without a "quick-fire" section such as this. Interviewees are expected to state a preference between two alternatives, which can be about practically any topic. Amazing drivel, lazy journalism or brilliant technique?

This way of measuring attitudes has long been known to psychologists. It's called *the catch-phrase technique* and was first derived to measure social attitudes such as conservatism.

In the late 1960s, Glenn Wilson, at the Institute of Psychiatry, devised a test to measure a person's conservatism. It was very simple and contained 50 items such as statements on the death penalty, evolution theory, patriotism, modern art and licensing laws. All the respondent had to do was to say "Yes," "Not sure" or "No" to indicate agreement or disagreement with the statement. Half of the statements referred to liberal ideas and practices, and half to conservative beliefs and behaviors. Thus a very convinced conservative would say "Yes" to one half of the items and "No" to the other half. Of course, in reality we are all somewhat incoherent, ambivalent and mixed in our ideas.

The catchphrase questionnaire may take only a few minutes and yield a simple score from one extreme X to the other extreme Y. One person's conservatism might be shown by looking at various attitudes such as Puritanism, anti-hedonism, punitiveness and a generalized intolerance.

To the sceptic and cynic, of course, the whole idea of measuring a political ideology in this way is scandalously preposterous. So the authors (Wilson and Patterson) of the first scale, published in 1968, asked volunteers to write long essays on specific topics that would easily reveal their liberal or conservative leanings. These were then read by political scientists and philosophers, who rated the writer's conservatism. They found to their glee that these scores correlated very highly with their catchphrase technique that had taken only moments to complete. So a good proxy can be obtained for a complex political philosophy in just a few minutes. Easy for the respondent; and accurate (enough) for the scientist.

Others developed similar measures of economic values. Was the respondent at heart a free-market capitalist or a socialist interventionist?

Again, catch-phrase technique results predicted party membership, voting patterns and so on.

So could this quick-fire, catch-phrase technique, used so commonly now in interviews, really reveal anything about an interviewee? As it stands, the answer appears to be negative. Most pose alternatives that are about essentially trivial issues such as food preferences or leisure activities or a liking for fashionable starlets of various kinds. They seem more an indication of awareness of modern popular culture than anything else.

Most obviously, the technique is open to unbridled impression management: in fact, a public relations dream. Get the agent on to it and they would easily advise the "correct" answer if the image one wants is "super cool" or "gravitas" or "quirky."

But the technique could be used to uncover some really deep-seated beliefs. Its advantage lies in what psychometricians call its ipsative nature: that is, a forced choice. This way of measuring attitudes is frequently used to prevent lying, dissimulation, faking or whatever you want to call it. Consider the choice: arrive at work late versus go home early; steal office stationery versus spend time on Facebook; bad-mouth your boss versus your colleagues. Or, if you prefer the other side: do voluntary work versus give to charity; take a pay cut versus work long hours.

To get something really useful out of the catch-phrase, quick-fire, technique you need to do three things. The *first* trick is to make the alternatives equally attractive or unattractive. It must be a difficult choice with no "obviously" good answer. The easier the choice, the more the flim-flammery. And make it really quick-fire. No time to contemplate or cogitate or coagulate. That means doing it live without any hesitation, repetition or deviation.

The *second* issue is to provide choices that relate to what you as an interviewer are interested in. If you are after political beliefs, choose items that speak to this: equality versus equity; bus pass versus heating allowance; national security versus freedom of information; pleasure versus self-restraint. You could also be a little more devious in tuning into areas related to those you are interested in. Tap into fundamental values (freedom, equality, law and order) and you pick up lots of "stuff."

The *third* issue is that the choices are updated not so much in being trendy or reflecting pop culture but rather the repackaging of old ideas. Some terms sound very dated: free collective bargaining, income policy and so on. But this does not mean having to be cutting-edge trendy.

There is another quick-fire technique that is rather less used at the time of writing. It is called sentence completion. In the jargon it is a "projective technique": the respondent projects his or her real self in a few lines. Typical would be completing the following:

I have always regretted..................................................................

My most conceited moment occurred when...........................................

The thing I most admire in others is...................................................

But it's plain to see that this is all too easy to fake.

Clever politicians and celebrities never give straight answers and hate the forced-choice nature of a good catch-phrase. All the more reason to use them.

## Reference

Wilson, G. and Patterson, J. (1968) "A New Measure of Conservatism," *British Journal of Social and Clinical Psychology*, 7: 264–8.

# Change

Funny how change agents and consultants are experts on changing systems, structures and other people, but rarely themselves. It is obviously a lot easier to attempt to change others or to change structures than to change oneself.

As a result of what psychologists call *"reduced plasticity"* most of us have stopped changing much by around 30 years old. What growth there is is often restricted to increasing girth, grey hair and wrinkles.

Most change is gradual, not dramatic and sudden. This is as true for weight gain and loss as it is the ability to gain and lose skills. And it is true of personal change: the way we think, feel and act. And that, alas is true when we try to change personal habits.

All coaches, counselors and therapists know that people change only if they want to. They cannot be forced or even bribed. They must really want change. So why would middle-aged people who are successful at work want seriously to change their life-style, philosophy and management style? There are half a dozen common causes:

1. *Loss*: Loss of a significant person (parent, spouse or child). This can, for some people, change the purpose of their life. All plans, hopes and dreams go with the lost person. The situation requires reappraisal. Less catastrophic, but also important, is the loss of a job. Sudden, unexpected and involuntary unemployment can have major consequences for the pattern of a person's life. But that destabilization is the "unfreezing" that can mean the beginning of change.
2. *Illness*: This is often caused by stress and habit disorders. The occasional headache, ulcer or sleepless night can be tolerated, but chronic stress is denied by most "toughies-at-the-top," though it easily manifests itself in psychosomatic disorders of various kinds. The stressed manager may self-medicate with "booze, bonking and baccy," but there is a cost. There is nothing like a health scare to make people take more than a pause in the rat-race of life. The Big C, a mild heart attack ... even angina can cause a serious reevaluation and an attempt to lead a better life.
3. *Insoluble conflict*: This as much outside as inside the workplace. Relationships are at the same time the major source of support and stress.

All relationships have rocky phases, but chronic, costly, seeming insoluble conflict with, say, a child, can make people ask for help and see the need for change. Being estranged from and ignored by children especially, but also old friends, is seriously hurtful.

4. *Unfulfilled dreams*: Most of us have career dreams, expectations and fantasies. A CEO by 35, retire at 40, three happy, healthy children. And as time ticks by it becomes apparent that the hope will probably never be fulfilled: will you ever make the board; become a professor/general/ judge? Failed hopes can induce grief, which can lead to a wake-up call.

5. *Inauthenticity*: Most people have to be "someone else" at work. Work requires a serious sacrifice of time commitment and so on. This can lead to a double life imbalance; a feeling that the game/sacrifice is not worth the candle/reward. This can go on for a long time.

6. *Trauma*: This may be of a life-threatening kind or not. Being involved in an accident, being robbed of precious possessions, or a brush with the law. This can shock people into a reappraisal of who they are, what they do, and – most important of all – what it all means.

So some enter therapy – oops......engage a business coach. Personal biography, personality and values will dictate what precisely they do. Some might try a spiritual retreat, others a rigorous expedition, but most seek guidance from some helping professional. The shame of mental illness and the taboo of anything prefaced by "psych-" means they would prefer someone like a coach, trainer or consultant.

And those personal versus organizational change agents will tell you that there are certain criteria or markers of what one might call change-readiness. In short, how much do they really want to change? Have they any understanding of the time, effort – and, yes, pain – of the journey? The hopes for the quick fix, silverbullet or magic potion must be squashed.

So what are the more hopeful characteristics? *First*, their psychological insight and curiosity, mainly about themselves but also about others. This is not an invitation to a narcissistic, self-indulgent self-justification fest. It is about trying to see connections between thoughts, emotions and behaviors in one's past and current life.

*Second*, emotional awareness and management: this is being affectively literate – able, willing and courageous enough to talk about true emotions. More than that, it is about how to deal with such emotions once the mud at the bottom of the pool is disturbed.

*Third*, the capacity for self-disclosure; that is, to open up to others, talk more openly and in a less guarded way about fears, beliefs and guilty secrets.

*Fourth*, receptivity and adaptability to the observations of others. This is about really listening to what has been said (usually many times).

It is true: if you always do what you've always done you will always get what you've always got. It is also true that change is a journey, not a destination. But sometimes we may be fortunate enough to be rattled out of our complacency and try something new. Even change agents themselves try to change.

# Charlatan detection

The word charlatan comes from the French, meaning sellers of medicines who might advertise their presence with music and an outdoor stage. Charlatans are people who make elaborate, fraudulent and often voluble claims to skill or knowledge they don't have; quacks or frauds. It has been said that journalists use the word guru as a polite synonym for charlatan when writing about the many self-appointed business experts.

You find them on daytime television, in the pages of low circulation magazines, and at conferences. Most are characterized by astonishing self-belief, theatrical gizmos and, most of all, tales of miracles that they alone can perform. These are usually about increasing profits, becoming rich and inheriting the earth.

But many have perfected the skills: the skills to persuade naïve, or perhaps desperate, business people.

In a famous paper, "Cold Reading," a psychologist called Ray Hyman (1977) revealed secrets of palmists, graphologists, fortune-cookie readers, and so on. The issue is how to persuade business clients of one's expertise. Many of the ideas are very useful.

Aspirant gurus take note:

1. *Remember that the key ingredient of a successful consultant is confidence.* If you look and act as if you believe in what you are doing, you will be able to sell. Strive to be viewed as a person with prestige or as someone who knows what he is doing.
2. *Make creative use of the latest fads, jargon, polls and surveys.* This can provide you with a wealth of material about what various subclasses of our society believe, do, want, worry about and so on.
3. *Set the stage for your presentation.* Profess a modesty about your talents. Make no excessive claims. This catches your subject off guard.
4. *Gain co-operation in advance.* Emphasize that the success of the whole enterprise depends as much upon a client's sincere cooperation as on the consultant's efforts. This ensures two invaluable ends: the guru has an alibi in case the diagnosis doesn't click: it's the client's fault, not the consultant's. And the clients will strive to fit the consultant's generalities to their specific life occurrences.

5. *Use any gimmick to hand.* Nowadays anything linked to the concept of neuroscience is great. It's all about how this new approach can and does get to the very heart of people issues.

6. *Have a list of stock phrases on the tip of your tongue.* A liberal sprinkling of attractive phrases amid your regular rambling will add depth to your insights.

7. *Keep your eyes open.* Try to size up a client on the basis of clothing, jewelry, mannerisms and speech. Listen for repeated phrases or the use of unusual terms. Watch the impact of your statements on the subject.

8. *Use the technique of "fishing."* This is simply a device for getting subjects to tell you about themselves, the team and the whole organization. Then you rephrase it and later feed it back. One version of fishing is to phrase each statement in the form of a question.

9. *Learn to be a good listener.* These are real psychiatric or counseling skills. Open-ended, big questions. Don't be afraid of silences. Act curious, puzzled, desperate to understand this unique problem. Most clients who seek the services of a business guru actually want someone to listen to their problems. In addition, many have already made up their minds about what choices they are going to make. They merely want support to carry out their own decisions.

10. *Dramatize your presentation.* Don't be afraid to "do emotions." Express horror and humor. Try to fit your style to theirs. Give back what little information you do have or pick up a little bit at a time. Make it seem more than it is. Build word pictures around each divulgence.

11. *Always give the impression that you know more than you are saying.* Once you persuade the client that you know one item of information about the issue, or the problem that you could not possibly have obtained through normal channels, the client will assume you know all. Don't be afraid to mention your qualifications, experience and expertise.

12. *Don't be afraid to flatter your subject with every chance you get.* Few will protest such flattery; most will revel in, and cherish, it. You can further flatter by saying, "You are always suspicious of people who flatter you."

13. *Finally, remember the golden rule: tell the client what he wants to hear.* They may have read of some dodgy idea or practice that promises a lot and delivers very little. If that is what they really want, say how good it is, how perspicacious the client is in knowing that is the best solution; and then charge like a wounded bull.

No wonder that clever, amoral psychopaths thrive as consultants of many sorts.

All consultants know they are in the relationship business. Many know the line between all the "c" words – consultant, coach, counselor – is paper-thin. They also know of the powerful and massive benefits of the placebo and the Hawthorne effect (see Furnham 2005) in any intervention.

## References

Furnham, A. (2005) *The Psychology of Behaviour at Work.* Hove: Psychologist Press.

Hyman, R. (1977) "Cold Reading: How to Convince Strangers that You Know All about Them," *The Zetetic* (now *The Skeptical Inquirer*), 1(2): 18–37.

# Child support

Many baby boomers complain that their children will not leave home. It's just too cosy and easy to have free accommodation, food and laundry provided. Four- and even five-star hotel facilities. Perhaps the children have been spoilt and as a result are not hardy or resilient enough to go out into the tough, cold, dog-eat-dog commercial world?

Where did they go wrong? Why are the children now not supporting their parents instead? Child support should be something you receive *from* your children after all the time, money and care you have lavished on them.

How to turn your child into a financially literate, serious and successful entrepreneur? We are told that CEO-ship starts in the playground, so how to encourage it? Are the younger generations narcissistic, entitled and indulgent, and quite unable to embrace the spirit of enterprise to become successful and self-sufficient?

What issues concern parents who want to make their children economically literate as well as entrepreneurial? Questions such as whether to attempt to turn shopping trips, even for pre-schoolers, into educational expeditions? When to start negotiating the rules for pocket money and allowances? Whether to reward good grades/marks at school with monetary rewards? How best to encourage sensible saving? When and how to open a bank account for them? Whether to get children interested in the stock market so as to raise a City of London/Wall Street whiz kid?

Whether to encourage one's children to do odd jobs (babysitting, gardening, cleaning) for friends, neighbors and/or strangers for money? What sort of part-time job, if any, should they seek? Whether to encourage voluntary (unpaid) work over paid work? Should family and friends give money or gifts for birthdays and other celebrations? How best to save, insure, invest money for them to secure a good future (for example, setting up trusts; reducing inheritance tax)? Whether to give or loan your university/college age children money for education, housing, cars and so on?

But the gurus can help. There are books of advice for parents. They are American, of course, and have titles such as *Raising Money-smart*

*Kids* or *Money Does Not Grow on Trees.* Here is their advice for children aged 7–12 years old:

- Get them into banking; formal savings. Explain how banks work. Go to the bank with them, read leaflets and open an account.
- Let them read about their investments, if they have any (bank statements/share certificates).
- Show them family bills (food, rent, insurance) and explain them fully.
- Explain issues like tipping, tolls, tokens, consumer rights, value-for-money, comparative shopping.
- Buy a consumer magazine and explain how it works.
- Watch television commercials or read ads in newspapers and magazines together and analyze them for motive, product value and technique.
- Explain tax (income and VAT) and tax your children's pocket money (say 10%) to have a family tax where the whole family both contributes and decides how to spend it. Family meetings should be called to discuss this.
- Lay down rules (with explanations) for borrowing, lending and trading, both within and outside the family.
- Explain the use of verbal and written contracts about money-related issues (that is, payback after loans).
- Establish rules/policies about breakages, money found on the street, mistaken over/under payments, shoplifting.

And for teenagers (13 years old and upwards):

- Encourage, model and educate them in the use of debit and credit cards.
- Encourage personal and internet banking. Discuss and calculate interest with them.
- Pay pocket money directly into their bank accounts, perhaps as a standing order.
- Make them personally and totally responsible for their own bills – especially clothes, mobile phones and computers.
- If you loan them money, agree and stick to reasonable repayment terms (period, interest).
- Charge them board if they have an income from part-time work.
- Encourage regular, sensible, thoughtful budgeting.

- Explain the stock market and together play with a set amount (such as £100). Start a portfolio, even at 13 or 14 years old.
- Show and explain family insurance policies, schemes and payments.
- Explain the concept of a will and the details of yours, specifically with respect to financial implications.
- Discuss your income honestly and how you spend it.
- Encourage smart consumerism: keeping receipts, knowing one's rights, understanding shop sales, knowing store return policies, reading the labels.
- Discuss entrepreneurship and opportunities to supplement income.
- Encourage your child to do part time (Saturday) jobs.
- Ask for evidence of budgeting plans and decisions.

Goodness! Makes the birds-and-bees talk look like a picnic. Indeed, have you ever had such a conversation with your spouse? My favorite was to tax their pocket-money at 10% to teach them about tax!

And what not to do? Ignore the whole topic through embarrassment, fear or ignorance? Avoid discussing money openly and honestly? Indulge your children through guilt, shame, laziness or any other problem? Send mixed messages about saving and spending, waste and profligacy? Putting money on the parental agenda is not easy, but it is worth it. It is odd that by the age of 12 most children know how to make babies, but not money.

# The content of job advertisements

Job ads: art-form, PR opportunity or information-giving device? It is said that people leave managers, not companies, and they seek jobs based, almost exclusively, on an organization's reputation and the salary, implied or specified. They make trade-offs: more dosh but a less prestigious organization; easier commuting for less salary; security of tenure for promotability. Titles are important too.

But most employers think they should also specify what qualities they are seeking: the attributes of the ideal or most suitable candidate. These may be based on the job description or not. They do give strong clues to how job applicants should "tweak their CVs" and present themselves at interview.

A content analysis of job advertisements presents an opportunity to ask and answer some interesting questions. *First*, what skills, traits or abilities are most often mentioned? And what is surprisingly rarely specified? *Second*, do different lists occur for junior versus senior jobs? And, related to this, are there differences in the public versus the private sector? *Third*, and perhaps most interesting, could you accurately guess the job title or the company (and the salary), if all you knew were the ideal attributes described?

The first thing to notice from the long list of attributes employers are looking for is that they are a curious mix of attitudes, dispositions and skills. Next, it is clear that different attributes are favored at different levels, and there do indeed seem to be observable differences between the public and private sectors.

By far the most common attribute required of private-sector jobs offering less than £60k per annum is *communication skills*. This term may be prefaced by *gifted*, *strong*, *unrivalled*, or *first-class*. Occasionally other similar concepts such as *articulate* or *good telephone manner* are added.

Two other "skills" are often mentioned in this group. The first is *organizational skills*, though it is not very clear what these are. The next is *leadership skill,* though that too is never unpacked.

These ads very often suggest they want *team players*, presumably meaning those who work well in groups. They also mention *highly motivated* – implying intrinsic rather than extrinsic motivation. Other words such as *self-starter*, *drive* and *commitment* are part of the same theme. *Success-driven* and *hungering for success* also occur.

Three other traits are often mentioned. One is *confident* and another *enthusiastic*. Other traits on this theme are *positive*, *dynamic* and *inspiring*. There are a surprising number of advertisements that mention *an eye for* or *meticulous attention to detail* or *accurate*.

There are also some quirky qualities mentioned: *sharp, nose for news, vibrant* and *bag of ideas*. Some things are rarely mentioned: *enterprising, entrepreneurial, work under pressure*.

The more prestigious positions of around £100k have some similarities. All that *competing, world-class, excellent communication skills* stuff remains very commonly discussed. But others emerge. Being *influential/ persuasive/diplomatic* often occurs. So does being *energetic* and *analytic, intellectually astute*. Here it is less about being motivated and more about being motivational.

The ads have a clear number of P words: *passionate, pragmatic, proactive, positive, persuasive, personable* and *politically astute*. The C words are *creative, clear thinking, credible, customer orientated, courageous, curious* and *culturally aware*. Some wanted *gravitas*, others *a holistic approach* and one mentioned *shrewd*.

And is the public sector any different? Jobs on £50k or under also most often mention *communication skills*. Equally commonly mentioned, predictably, are *organizational* and *management skills*, but three C words were included very frequently: *co-operative, creative* and *committed*. *Ambitious* was mentioned a number of times as well.

For the more senior public sector staff, the pattern was very clear. One attribute, *strategic/thinking/vision*, surpassed even *communication skills* in the number of mentions, followed by *effective leadership*. There were the usual odd phrases: *a champion of the department, strength of character, not happy to sit still, behavior consistent with values*.

Studying the job ads may really help applicants (and recruiters). They can craft their CVs to the attributes required. Ads also say a lot about the state of the organization and its values: how it works, what it lacks, and what is important to it.

Intelligence is certainly one of the key predictors of work success, but is mentioned only occasionally (*intellectual, rigor, smart*). This may have something to do with the legal position on discrimination, however.

*Emotional adjustment* or *neuroticism* hardly get a look in. Only three of the 600 ads studied mentioned *stress-resistant person*; one mentioned *calm*, and another *works well under pressure*. Emotional stability is one of the best predictors of work success, yet is hardly considered. It predicts absenteeism, decision-making ability and energy levels consistently.

No one mentioned the work ethic or conscientiousness, though features of it such as *ambition*, *dependable* and *reliable* appeared. Conscientiousness is the single best personality trait predictor of school, college and work results. It is of crucial importance.

And the characteristic people always and everywhere most want in their boss? Integrity – which did not receive a single mention, nor any linked concept such as morality.

It is no wonder the emotional intelligence concept became so popular, given the mentions of *communication* and *people skills*. Yet all ads tend to list three to five skills: *leadership*, *organizational*, *influence*, *communication* and *negotiation*. How, when and where are these best acquired?

Why not make the job ad the job description? That makes it harder for the candidate: they have to infer the qualities required.

# Could do better

In the old days (read 30-plus years ago) before political correctness, litigious lawyers and pushy parents, teachers used to write exactly what they thought on school reports (as did doctors in their patients' notes).

The observations were pithy and poignant. They usually represented the astute observations of no-nonsense teachers who had the measure of the pupils in their classrooms. Indeed, they may well have known considerably more about the children than did their parents, particularly the fathers, whose interactions with their children were "as brief as possible" and somewhat functional.

It is not uncommon for biographers to seek out and print the school reports of celebrities such as politicians, artists and entertainers. Further, these are occasionally collected into amusing "lavatory" books for quick edification and delight. One such title, edited by Catherine Hurley (2002), is subtitled *School Reports of the Great and the Good*.

The school reports fall essentially into three categories. The first shows the remarkable prescience of teachers who get to the heart of a child. They see real talent, whether it is explored or exploited or not. The second is precisely the opposite, where some now widely recognized genius was considered a complete dullard at school, completely bereft of talent. The third illustrates the now practically illegal, caustic sniping of a world-weary Mr M'Choakumchild in Charles Dickens' *Hard Times*.

Here are some accurate assessments of well-known people, all derived from the book. *Peter Cook*: "No doubt about ability, but disappointed that he does not make more use of it." *Jeremy Paxman*: "His stubbornness is in his nature, and could be an asset when directed to sound ends." *Princess Diana*: "She must try to be less emotional in her dealings with others." *Winston Churchill*: "Is in constant trouble and is always in some scrape or another."

Some inaccurate assessments: *Eric Morecambe*: "This boy will never get anywhere in life." *John Lennon*: "Certainly on the road to failure … hopeless."

The Old School: *Diana Rigg*: "She has been very tiresome in the dormitory this term." *Stephen Fry*: "He has glaring faults and they have certainly glared at him this term." *Jilly Cooper*: "She has set herself an extremely low standard which she has failed to maintain." *Robert Graves*: "Remember that your best friend is the waste paper basket." *Field Marshal*

*Bernard Montgomery*: "Sometimes strange … backward … No notion of style." *Michael Heseltine*: "He is rebellious, objectionable, idle, imbecilic, inefficient, antagonizing, untidy, ludic, albino, conceited, conceived, inflated, impertinent, underhand, lazy and smug."

To this day, however, the theme of "could do better" pervades school reports. What the various synonymous phrases all imply is that output – in the form of school results – are partly the result of effort, which can be increased.

Three factors play a large part in determining "life trajectories": ability, effort and luck. The latter refers to being in the right place at the right time, choosing your parents well, and general serendipity. Ability, now sometimes called talent, has to be discovered. Some people are multiply endowed; others very sparsely. It's not fair, but there it is.

The factor we can control, however, is effort. Much of the content of socialization both at school and in the home is about teaching conscientiousness: being reliable, dependable and organized. It's about pitching up and pitching in, even when you don't feel like it. It's about postponing pleasure until the work is done.

Ability is wasted without effort. Effort can even make up for ability, as in the concept of the "plodder" and the "swot." Other ways of achieving success are ingratiation – being a "teacher's pet" – and even the sabotage of the really talented through character assassination and so on.

Parents and teachers know that some pupils are easier to mould than others. The business of instilling or awakening the conscience is a slow and difficult but vitally important business. Others respond weakly.

There is something particularly sad about seeing wasted talent. This occurs when people with great gifts are unable or unwilling to exploit them. Some, with what has been called the imposter syndrome, actually self-handicap, and often turn to drink or drugs in an attempt to cope.

For some, the game is not worth the candle. The effort required does not match the reward given over the attraction of the alternatives to that effort.

But, of course, there is also *too much* effort. It's called workaholism. Huxley described a fanatic as a man who consciously overcompensates for a secret doubt. And the workaholic is indeed a sad person, trying by massive, often pointless, effort to achieve some peace of mind and self-worth.

But "could do better" is a lot more optimistic than "can't do better." The latter in some way suggests there is nothing in reserve: the pedal is already flat to the floor.

The secret of most schooling is, or should be, to fire enthusiasm and interest that is connected to abilities and skills. To find that you are captivated by an activity at which you show talent, is sheer heaven. It turns work into play, drudgery into passion.

The problem at school is the compulsory subjects. Fortunately, in life we take electives. Happy is the man or woman who finds his or her talents early. For s/he could never be required to "do better."

## Reference

Hurley, C. (2002) *Could Do Better: School Reports of the Great and the Good.* London: Pocket Books.

# The dangers of forecasting

It is always interesting, when speculating on the future in areas such as the world of work, health provision or climate change, to examine the success of past prognosticators. Indeed, the whole process of predicting future trends, even based on sound empirical sources, is inherently difficult, given that quite unexpected and novel occurrences (inventions, wars, economic crises) with substantial and wide-ranging effects can upset the most reasonable, rational forecasts. Many forecasts have been wrong: the 20-hour week, the paperless office, the leisure economy, to name but a few contemporary predictions.

Forecasting the future is a difficult business, as the following quotations show:

*"This telephone has too many shortcomings … as a means of communication … the device is inherently of no value."*
(Western Union internal memo, 1876)

*"The light bulb … unworthy of the attention of practical or scientific men."*
(British Parliamentary Committee, 1883)

*"Heavier than air flying machines are impossible."*
(Lord Kelvin, President, The Royal Society, 1895)

*"Everything that can be invented has been invented."*
(US Office of Patents, 1899)

*"Airplanes are interesting toys but of no military value."*
(Marshal Foch, Professor of Strategy, Ecole Supérieure de Guerre (1911)

*"Who the hell wants to hear actors talk?"*
(Harry Warner, Warner Bros, 1927)

*"I think there is a world market for maybe five computers."*
(Thomas Watson, Chairman of IBM, 1943)

*"Space travel is utter bilge".*
(Richard van der Riet Woolley, British Astronomer Royal, 1956)

*"There is no reason for any individuals to have a computer in their home."*

(Ken Olsen, President and Founder of Digital Equipment Corporation, 1977)

It is no different in the world of health forecasting. There are two essential methods for estimating the future. The first is *extrapolation:* this involves looking for trends. The second is *"what ifs"*: this involves "blue sky" thinking.

The *extrapolation* school have seen the future as involving greater patient mobility and "information-hungry" patients; patients demanding to see and own their personal medical data; patient demands for all new prescription medicines; a vast growth in medical tourism; an increasing complexity of health insurance determining who pays for what; and an increasing need for better health education resulting from the essential failure of past attempts. The absolute necessity of rationing will cause many ethical and moral dilemmas. The spread of epidemics will be faster than ever before because of the ease of travel. There will be new political pressure on drug pricing. Places of work will be required to establish their own health agendas.

Those who have worked in the *"what if"* school have asked questions such as: What if your health data was to be available at any time, and in any place? What if you could have brain surgery for weight loss? What if new technologies allowed us to experience the full future effects of our current misbehavior?

But what about work? Richard Donkin (2010) has argued that today's world of work is changing as quickly and dramatically as it did at the time of the Industrial Revolution. Changing technology, living patterns and attitudes to work have altered where, how and why we work as we do. Donkin identified a number of themes, or forces, that have shaped, and will continue to shape, the future of work:

1. *Demographics*: In the West, this means fewer young people relative to a large aging population who are, very expensively, living longer. This has led to attempts to add to the numbers of younger people by immigration, which has resulted in a diversified workplace. In the future, people will be healthier than ever before and with a significantly increased longevity. This will affect the whole concept of retirement: whether it should be mandatory; whether people should be expected to

work into their seventies. Governments and private companies simply will not be able to finance the pension levels of the past.

2. *Health*: For obvious reasons, organizations want to encourage a (physically and mentally) healthy workforce. Employers will provide health care and fitness facilities, which are a good investment and potentially attractive to many employees.

3. *Working women*: The workplace and workforce have been *feminized*, which has led to conflict between production and reproduction.

4. *Technological advances*: These have been both a scourge and a savior at work. Electronic means of communication such as Facebook, the Blackberry and the internet in general have changed dramatically how, when and where we make contact with fellow workers and customers. Thus it will be the technologically adept rather than the great orators who will be particularly influential in the future.

5. *Social networking* This has changed contact patterns both inside and outside the workplace and makes secrets much harder to control. The quality and quantity of a person's connections will inevitably influence his/her work productivity and capability.

6. *Authenticity at work*: People will seek more meaning, purpose and authenticity in their work. They will not blindly accept the values and career paths of previous generations and will ask serious questions about what they have inherited and what they will pass on to others.

7. *Business leaders*: They will be more in the spotlight. In particular, they will have to adapt to the demands of the new and ever-changing order.

8. *Performances measurement*: There will be changes in how people's performance is measured at work. People will be evaluated more frequently and more subtly, both qualitatively and quantitatively.

9. *Working hours*: There will be shorter formal working hours and more discretion for workers to decide when they are working.

All these predictions seem entirely reasonable, given current demographics, technology, economy and social order. Will they turn out to be correct, or look as ridiculous as those historical examples? Only time will tell.

### Reference

Donkin, R. (2010) *The Future of Work*, Basingstoke: Palgrave Macmillan.

# Different perspectives

Despite the best efforts of the matrix-management gurus, people still show strong tribal loyalty at work. And no surprise there: we become architects or accountants, marketers or microbiologists because of our abilities, our values and our personal preferences. And we find we end up happily working with people like us. We are by definition alike; we like each other and we like our silos the way they are.

Silos develop mini-corporate cultures. You see it in the way people in their department or building dress and speak; in their funny, fetishistic rituals and their after-work activities. They are for the modern anthropologist as clearly a tribe as are a primitive people living in a distant land. They are happy living together, and the more isolated their building or territory the more different they become over time.

Organizations on split sites can suffer interesting problems. The financial team sent to a cheaper building in a dreary suburb or the HR group posted to a provincial backwater feel isolated and forgotten, like some colonial island in the middle of a big sea. On the other hand, it often has a powerful and beneficial effect on their sense of identity, making them feel they are an elite corps, essential to all aspects of the business.

The problems associated with homogenous groups working together is that, because they share similar strengths and weaknesses ... oops, *developmental opportunities*, they tend to be very good at some things but rather poor at others. And they play to their strengths. Added to this is the rather idiosyncratic and blinkered view they have of themselves and others.

Psychologists call this a fundamental attribution error. Things are attributed to one's own group very differently from another group. *We* succeed through personal effort and ability; *they* by luck, favoritism and corruption. We fail because the system and the forces of darkness and fate are against us at this particular time; *they* fail because they simply have not got what it takes.

So, warm and cosy in a silo, we look out at others in the same organization and see very different things. Over time we have a view of ourselves somewhat different from the way others see us.

Consider, for example, four groups – finance, marketing, production and human resources.

### Finance

Finance people are analytical and detail oriented. They understand the business; where the wires go; what comes in and goes out; when, where and why. Many pride themselves in their strategic thinking. But turning ideas into action is quite another thing. Most are very poor at influencing line managers and getting the results they so carefully detail.

And their view of themselves? Prudent protectors of profit, careful custodians of company cash and meticulous monitors of mistakes. Other groups, they think, would bankrupt the company in days if it were not for their wise and shrewd decisions.

But those other groups see them as bureaucratic, obsessive "nyet-men" who lack vision, don't understand customers (particularly of the internal type) and crush innovation.

### Marketing

Marketing people are action-oriented: they sure get things done. They are also well-known for being entrepreneurial and resourceful and quite naturally risk takers. But their quirky individualism means they struggle with teamwork, ignore corporate systems and tend to be very inconsistent.

Marketers see themselves as swashbuckling, visionary, just-do-it types who understand the future. They see themselves as creative, adaptive and forward-looking, fighting those too stuck in the past or present.

But others often see them as naïve airheads with little sense of reality, wasteful, gimmicky bullshitters, enthusiastic for every passing phrase.

### Production

Operations-driven people know all about efficiency and teamwork. They use systems well and their eye is on execution. But they often don't change and don't always see the big picture. Equally, many respond poorly to internal customers.

The production group see themselves as hard-working and uncomplaining but unrecognized and pitifully compensated people who make the whole damn thing happen. They believe they are constantly frustrated and dictated to by finance, marketing and sales, who have no understanding of the production process and who demand whimsical changes and cost-cutting all the time.

And the view of others? Obstructive, obstreperous, obdurate techies with no understanding of the changing and capricious world of customer demands. They are slow non-adapters, obsessed by schedules and control processes that impede company success.

### Human resources

HR people rejoice in their teamwork and often their persuasiveness. They can, out of necessity, be very resourceful. And they master the techniques appropriate to their area. But many are deeply risk adverse. And, paradoxically, though they talk a lot about it, and even run courses on it, leadership is not their strong suit.

They see themselves as the heart (but not head) of the organization. The people who guard the most valuable asset – people. Some believe they are the guardians of morale and engagement, which, of course, drives productivity. The puzzle is why the head of HR does not sit on the board.

Others see HR as measurement obsessed overall; and concerned with pointless form-filling. They see all HR processes, particularly appraisal, as backfiring time-wasting activities designed to drive a wedge between management and employees.

To translate Robert Burns, from the Scottish dialect: "Oh, would some power the gift give us/To see ourselves as others see us."

# Does coaching work?

It is easy to be skeptical, indeed cynical, about executive coaches. The sacked, sour and and screwed-up executive one day becomes the executive coach the next. But this is clearly more than a fad or fashion that disappears by the end of the fiscal year. It is a massive growth industry, even if supply seems to have exceeded demand.

The growth in the mental health professions over the last 25 years in most developed countries has been spectacular. And those paying for these services have also been clamoring to rationalize the expense by showing that treatment really is effective. What, they ask, is the active ingredient? If, of course, there is one?

Academics have tried to provide both an answer and a percentage; that is, how important is each explanatory factor. Interestingly, the four factors apply (roughly) equally to all forms of counseling, therapy, coaching or whatever the help is called.

First, client factors. It is, in short, more important to know who (what kind of person) has the problem than what the problem is. This accounts for a whopping 40 percent of the effect. It is accurately reflected in the old joke "How many psychologists does it take to change a light bulb? Answer: only one. But the light bulb needs to want to be changed."

It's called *readiness for coaching*. It is a mixture of being willing and able to learn, to change, to embrace challenge. The coach needs to assess and then stimulate readiness, remove barriers and resistance to moving on. Further, the professional needs to respond to the clients' preferences. Some (they are called internalizers) want insight, others (called externalizers) want symptom-focused approaches. Much depends on whether the client is a conscript or a volunteer; and if the latter, for what do they think they are signing up? This is why there is a first meeting, prior to the "sign up" session.

There is a bit of a paradox here. If 40 percent of the success of coaching comes from client dispositions then coaches can, at most, take only 60 percent of the credit for the magic they perform. So it's dangerous for the coach to develop hubris. Some clients are eminently coachable (however much you do) and others are not. Often, those who need it the most resist it most vigorously, and vice versa.

Ingredient two: it's the *relationship,* stupid. The coach can explore and exploit the therapeutic alliance. It's about collaboration, consensus and support. It's the effective and affective bond. Again, this has to be tailored to the client. It is about building and maintaining a positive, open, productive and, one hopes, transformative alliance.

However, it should be pointed out that it is the client's and not the coach's explanation of the alliance that is important: coaches need to check this fact regularly with their clients. The distracted, fatigued or unprepared coach is a poor coach. The alliance is usually based on set and agreed goals and tasks.

The third ingredient that buys you 15 percent of the result is that old-fashioned quality sometimes called hope, now called *expectations*. It is about the expectation of improvement, finding new paths to goals and "agency thinking:" the belief that one can if one tries.

Coaches speak and leak the message that successful change or progress is possible. They actuate hope by credibility building at the beginning of the relationship. Clients can detect loss of faith in the project by the coach.

And the final ingredient is the application of every/any theory and therapy; The use of healing rites and rituals. It accounts for 15 percent of the power of coaching. The coaches' backgrounds influence their focus. While some look at organizational competition, conflict, dominance and power, others may look at self-awareness and encourage personal SWOTS: the old standards Strengths, Weaknesses, Opportunities and Threats.

Theories organize observation. Some coaches share them with their clients, while others don't. Clearly, the good coach needs to know what works for whom. But coaches also need to know about the business world and the dilemma of conflict of interests between the client and the organization. Coaches really have to be business savvy. They need to read the *Financial Times*, not Freud; and *The Economist*, not Erikson.

The client–coach mission and relationship is a bit like the patient–therapist one. But there are differences. Typically, patients have more serious problems and poorer adjustment than do business clients. Therapists work at a deeper emotional level than a coach. Therapists see more of the patient and contact is nearly always face-to-face. Coaches focus on the workplace, while therapists concentrate on all aspects of functioning.

Patients often seek personal growth and the alleviation of suffering, while coaching clients want enhanced work performance. Coaching clients seek to enhance their emotional intelligence, political prowess and understanding of cultural differences.

So there we have it. Coaching only works if the client is able, ready and willing. It works well if the bond is good, and if the coach instills hope for change. Would an internal mentor do just as well? Perhaps. But the external, unbiased objectivity of an outside coach is often preferred.

Are some executives uncoachable? Clearly. Is coaching worth the money? Sometimes.

# The drive for money

The statistic that many people, particularly economists, find difficult to swallow relates to the Easterlin Hypothesis. Note "hypothesis", not "law." It's quite simple and the central question is "How much money do you need to be happy?" The answer is (only) about £40–50K per annum. After that you get no "hedonic bang for your buck." So why do so many people chase money so remorselessly and so relentlessly? And at what cost? Do they not believe the statistic? Do they believe not only that greed is good, but also that it buys health, happiness and hedonism?

What are people prepared to forfeit for the almighty dollar? What is worth the sacrifice? The answer is threefold, and what is particularly interesting is the paradox in the whole business.

Perhaps our most valuable asset, a finite resource, is *time*. The older we get, the more we know that to be true. Time is irretrievable. We have our three score years and ten. You can't take it with you. There are no pockets in a shroud.

And yet to buy time for leisure one has to sacrifice it in business. Long days become long years. Holidays are shortened. Work is done on holiday. And it saps one's energy, enthusiasm and life-force.

Who was it that said that life is like a bank account that offers only withdrawals, no deposits? You can't deposit sleep or time. It's finite.

And, yes, the fantasy it to make a pile of money and to retire early to a life of leisure. But the slog transforms people. They experience burnout. They can't be playful or creative any more; life is grim and life is earnest. Work is all-consuming. It means for some that they are never able to experience real recreational leisure again.

The second sacrifice is linked to the first: it is *mental and physical health*. Sure, you can buy private medicine, psychotherapy and spa treatments. But long working hours, a rich diet, few exercise opportunities and work stresses take their toll. Top executives often experience an array of psychosomatic illnesses, from migraine to irritable bowel syndrome as a result of chronic stress.

Hardly an ideal situation, working oneself to death. To sacrifice health for money and then to try and buy it back again.

But there is a third cost, more subtle but perhaps even more costly than the previous two. It is the forfeiting of one's *integrity*, *reputation and kindness.* You have to be tough, wily and even callous in business to succeed. You have to kick ass, beat your adversaries, and duck and weave around tax laws.

Not all successful people compromise their principles, but on the way up only the most ruthless do well. Perhaps that is why so many seem to try to buy their way out of an imagined purgatory by giving vast fortunes away later.

It is true that money can't buy love, happiness or health, but it has two other real allures. The first is best known as "**** off" money. It's the ability to tell anybody, anywhere, to go away. Money is freedom. You are no longer beholden to bosses, shareholders, parents or spouses.

Money is freedom: not only from want, but also from the capricious demands, whim and dictates of others. Many rich, successful people experienced first-hand or saw in their parents the powerlessness that poverty brings. Seeing the parents' constant struggle to survive: to have to give up dignity and health to please others. This is a serious driver of wealth accumulation.

The second major attraction of money is also not what material things it can buy, but rather it's a way of keeping score. It's very simple, very objective, very clean.

It's not really how much one has absolutely, but how much relative to significant others: pompous, patronising, privileged acquaintances from school or university; siblings who seemed cleverer, or taller or more handsome; and former colleagues who did well.

Money means success. It is the best measure of success. And therefore it boosts self-esteem and a sense of self-worth. Indeed, for some it is worth having just because it puts others' noses out of joint. Nothing like being envied. Money doesn't talk; it shouts, it swears, it says "Hah, look at me!"

Money shows you have made it. You have triumphed over adversity and won the race. You have literally earned self-esteem.

Once you begin to play the game you are trapped. If money is your major source of self-esteem you will never be released from the treadmill.

And money makes you less trusting. To what extent are people polite, amused by your jokes and very complimentary about your appearance because they are simply sycophantic, fawning money grabbers? Can you buy respect or friendship? Alas not.

Happiness can't be bought. To some extent it is a trait: a habitual positiveness; a way of gaining social support from others. Possessions count for little; but experiences for a great deal.

So why the manic, fanatical, addictive drive for money? It is part of the culture. But the fairy tales also very clearly state that it's a false God and that those who chase it will only derive any real happiness from giving it away.

Remember £50K. That's enough.

# The emotional contract at work

It has been common to differentiate between two types of contract at work. First, there is the legal contract. This is the ever-lengthening, and complicated, piece of paper that one signs on accepting a job. It sets out to measure and subtly legalize the roles, requirement and obligations of both parties concerning all salient aspects of the work. It is an important document that is only really studied carefully by most job-holders before unfair dismissal tribunals.

The other contract is usually not written down. And that is part of the problem. It is based on a set of implicit assumptions and expectations on the part of the individual employee at all levels. But, unlike the legal contract, it is very fluid and flexible, being relatively – indeed surprisingly – easy to change. It is fragile.

The psychological contract is essentially concerned with a set of expectations and obligations. Employees come to believe, based on the organization's PR sent out in vision/mission and other statements, including their job advertisements and the application process, that they are being offered various things, such as: security of employment; promotion prospects and opportunities; training and development programmes; help and care in times of trouble; and being treated fairly and with dignity.

And employees usually offer something in return: a soft form of conformity and obedience: obeying the rules and abiding by the requirements of the job and the instructions of supervisors. They also offer loyalty by staying on in the job, perhaps when they have had attractive offers from elsewhere. And, linked to this, they offer commitment.

Employees offer trust in response to the trust they feel has been invested in them. So they feel they will keep their promises if the organization does likewise. Rather than "bad mouth" their boss and the organization, some employees feel it is part of the deal to show loyalty. Further, they don't take part in a whole range of underhand behaviors such as stealing, sabotage, vengeful whistle-blowing and dishonest absenteeism.

And this amorphous, nebulous yet crucially important concept is clearly linked to a person's motivation, satisfaction and well-being at work. It is both a cause and a consequence. If an employee's contract is honored, it is likely (but not certain) that he or she will be happy and satisfied at work.

There is a threefold problem for the employer with the psychological contract. *First*, it is not a standard contract, and people having identical jobs and with much the same experience may *differ widely* in their hopes, expectations and sense of obligation. The expectations of a deeply entitled "Y Generation" employee may be quite different from that of a working-class baby boomer, say.

It has been suggested that many of the latest generation have a quite different sense of entitlement from their parents. They are less respectful of authority but demand much more respect themselves. They emphasize the opposite of the spirit of President Kennedy's great speech: "Ask not what you can do for your organization but rather what it can do for you!"

Do the sexes differ in their hopes, expectations and thus their contracts? Certainly there is enough data to suggest that men and women value things rather differently at work. And there must be cultural and ethnic differences in the perception and experience of work.

And, of course, personalities and values. Those with poor emotional adjustment may value secure interpersonal relationships more than those hardy, stable and resilient individuals happy to face the slings and arrows of misfortune. Those with what Americans call "negative affectivity" want, need and expect less conflict, less time pressure and fewer demands at work. And the less conscientious expect to do the minimum of work, while those with a strong work ethic are usually happy to go the extra mile.

All this makes the psychological contract very difficult to manage. And if it's true that you can only manage what you can measure, then the unmeasured, implicit feeling that is the psychological contract is unmanageable.

*Second*, there is the problem of the *fragility* of the psychological contract. Often "by accident" and possibly without even noticing, an employer can "break" its contracts with employees. Little things can have big consequences in the perception of employees. A nasty comment made in jest or in anger can take on great significance for the poorly adjusted, oversensitive employee. A good contract can become a bad one in an instant.

This is particularly difficult for managers, as they have to take into account wide individual differences in the workplace. While some might find the content of a joke amusing, others might be deeply offended.

*Third*, the psychological contract may be about ideas and expectations, but the emotional contract is even more problematic. We are people of the head and people of the heart. And these are connected. Some of us are better regulated emotionally than others.

While all managers should attempt to clarify and manage employees' expectations about what they give and get, few receive much instruction in emotional intelligence, which is defined simply as an awareness of one's own and others' emotions and the ability to manage them.

# Esthetics at work

What values do the art and architecture of organizations communicate? How much PR and advertising value do you get from your organizational exteriors and interiors? What is real value of having an iconic building?

You can communicate many things from your building and its interior: state-of-the-art, cutting-edge science; an eye for classical beauty; orderly, conservative solemnity or pragmatic utilitarianism. Now, of course, you get extra "hero-points" for being super-clean and green with all that carbon metric sophistry.

And even if the outside is dull, drab and dreary you can certainly do something about the inside. Modern art, water-features, wide-open, expensive spaces. Should there be fresh flowers, free coffee and newspapers ... and if so, which? There are, after all, olfactory esthetics.

What about the design of the reception area: is it to be more like a five-star hotel or a border crossing point? Are you conveying success or security? What does the waiting area convey: a TV channel permanently on a finance channel, or a modernist sculpture in a zen-like quiet space? Does it have clocks, and if so, showing which time(s) ... New York, Hong Kong or Peckham?

While some buildings have an iconic value (the Hoover Building, the Lloyds Building, the Gherkin) some organizations seem quite happy to work in dull, functional buildings. Visit Tesco's versus Sainsbury's headquarters and you experience some contrast. The former is located in a side-street of a smallish town (Cheshunt) 30 minutes from London, while the latter makes a statement in glass in Holborn, yards away from the City of London.

Buildings make statements about those who inhabit them: their wealth, values, taste. But so does the way they are decorated, including everything from the color schemes to the gardening. How to show that you are "environmentally aware," whether you care (or not) about the diet of your staff (and visitors), and the extent to which you are aware of safety issues.

And if you are an environmental determinist, buildings affect the very behavior taking place in them. Consider how the House of Commons perpetuates the two-party system, or the British Airways Waterside building keeps people in it (to do shopping!). We shape our buildings and afterwards they shape us.

Some (very successful) banks' and solicitors' offices embrace conspicuous consumption: large empty spaces in places that command some of the highest space-rates in the world. Some do modern art or sculpture, while other organizations are so concerned with security that the first things you see are barriers and bouncer-like characters dressed in ill-fitting suits and standing in macho positions.

There is an academic literature on esthetic preference: preference for art and music; film and poetry; architecture and dance. Each area has its genre, which acts as a convenient category scheme for researchers. So you can ask (the aesthetically literate) whether they prefer Cubism over Surrealism, or Fascism over Romanticism in art; what they think about Art Deco buildings, or their taste in jazz.

Some art forms are taken seriously by organizations. Try to notice the effect of music at work. Shops use music to change mood and pace, as do restaurants. Music is played while you are "on hold." Restaurants play music for "effect." There is music in stores. We still have "music while you work" in those almost obsolete, dull manufacturing jobs.

But what music: fast or slow, modern or classical, vocal or instrumental, minor or major key? For some, like buskers, their livelihood is determined by it. Quiz them and see if "their take" is affected by time-of-day $\times$ musical interactions. That is, does the same music played at different times of the day have a radically different effect on the amount of coins thrown into the hat? Should one play different music at upmarket tube stations (such as Hampstead)? Does the saxophone yield more profit than the guitar? People research this stuff because it really makes a difference.

But what about the visual arts? You are about to commission a design for a new headquarters building, perhaps in a big city or on more land outside the town. You expect many important people to visit your building. It may even lead on to a new logo or a new letterhead. You want it to communicate your values. How do you brief the architect?

And once it is built, how do you decorate it inside? How do you best use the space to communicate what you believe it can stand for? And how much freedom do you give individuals to personally choose art for their space. Wandering around Dilbert cubicles, one is often struck by the desperation of the semi-imprisoned inhabitants to bring beauty into their world.

So which department is responsible for the esthetics? Does it fall into some pretty unlikely gaps like Estates and Parks and PR? Why is there no Chief Esthetics Office? Because this is all too petty, trivial and time-wasting?

Buildings do influence interaction patterns: its pretentiously called propinquity. And we get to know those whom we like, bump into and see most often at work. So we can engineer desilofication if we choose. But the esthetics of the environment impacts on mood and morale, which maybe more important.

# Evidence at work

The medics probably started it. Then it became all the rage, and "evidence-based" medicine was soon followed by evidence-based education, management, policing and policy-making. In HR, the prefix "evidence-based" is now as favored as the suffix "intelligence" in HR – "emotional intelligence," "negotiating intelligence," "practical intelligence."

Of course, it comes as a serious surprise to many that medicine wasn't "evidence-based" in the first place. If not evidence, then what on earth was it based on? Old wives' tales, magic, hocus-pocus? Or pet theories of doctors and hospital administrators?

There are stories of how dramatically different approaches can be. Russian babies are swaddled tight, turning them into towelled dolls. Imitating the tight confines of the womb they had just left, it gave them profound comfort (and warmth). American babies were encouraged to have naked body contact with their mothers to facilitate bonding. Both approaches made sense. Both had been done for decades. Practice made perfect, or so it seemed.

But did the Russian method encourage helplessness in babies and make it difficult to establish a relationship with their mothers? Were American babies particularly prone to self-harm or chills? No one knew, because no one had tested the theory. Doing so would involve taking a large number of similar babies (sex, birth conditions, age of mother and so on) and giving half the American and half the Russian treatment. Does it make any difference? If so, what, when and why? Could the practice explain the Russian love of vodka or the American obsession with large (milk-laden) breasts? A ridiculous idea, or an issue worth serious investigation? Longitudinal research, of the sort required to answer the question, is very expensive and thus rarely done. So the practice becomes one based on beliefs and tradition, not evidence.

And it's the same story in offices and classrooms. Some practices are simply repeated because they seem to work without any evidence to support them. Corporal punishment taught self-discipline and kept discipline, then it was considered barbarous, humiliating and encouraged violence. One generation's wise practice becomes the next's laughable nonsense.

And what of all those fads in business? Did open-plan offices improve communication, or was that just a clever way to reduce office space? And what about the current fads? Are fully-engaged people really more productive? Are emotionally intelligent managers more successful? Are appraisals essential at work? Where is the good (clear, unchallenged) evidence that any of this is true?

Indeed, practices sometimes seem to be consultant-based or guru-based rather than evidence-based. Someone with confidence, an MBA or able to tell modern parables, said it was so and people believed it. There was fad-based practice: decentralization, recentralization, process reengineering. Nothing to do with evidence and everything to do with following the fad-based management of others. Or desperation-based evidence.

There are at least three reasons why so many work-based practices are not evidence-based. The *first* is cost. It is said it now costs around £1 million to do a proper evidence-based evaluation of some herbal remedy, say a tea that supposedly causes weight-loss or a substance that reduces hay fever, migraines or palpitations. And multiply that by 10 for a new drug. To scientifically test the efficacy of a practice or process takes time, effort and money. Things that seem to work are repeated without any real evidence that they do. They may work through the placebo effect or as a self-fulfilling prophecy. They may make no difference at all. And they may actually impede productivity, efficiency and well-being at work. We simply don't know.

The *second* reason for not advocating an evidence-based approach is that too many people have a vested interest in selling snake-oil ointments, silver-bullet science and evidence-free solutions to expensive, complex problems. Gurus don't want their authority challenged by inconvenient truths. Consultants often don't like investing in proof.

Research evidence might show that whole departments should be made redundant. What if it were shown that health and safety practices backfired and actually increased risk and danger? What if the psychometric tests used for selection were shown to be both unreliable and invalid? What if the new computer system worked less efficiently than the old one? And what if the evidence suggested that one person could do the work of three in half the departments?

*Third*, the evidence may suggest a practice that is illegal or deeply frowned upon by the politically correct police, the PR department or the litigation-avoiding manager. What if the evidence points to sex or race differences in productivity at work? What if it was shown that overweight people were more often absent, slower and less happy than their slimmer colleagues?

You can see how scientists are treated who even dare to investigate certain topics let alone show that some quite unacceptable "facts" are true. So evidence is suppressed, ignored and those who "produce" it are stigmatized, attacked and ostracized.

So evidence-based management is not without its problems and clearly could be a two-edged sword in some circumstances. But, as the old adage has it, "If you think research is expensive, try ignorance." Under what circumstances could one honestly not want evidence-based proof for practices at work?

# Expansion

There is a funny yet poignant email presentation going the rounds. It is a modern allegory about the expansive nature of staff roles in organizations. Well, funny is not really the right word. It presents a horrid truth in a cartoon style. The viewer is left with a wry smile: it would be funny if it were not true.

It begins with a happy, productive ant, whose boss, the Big Lion, discovers the ant does not have a proper supervisor. So a cockroach is appointed to the role and he sets up an office with the necessary computers to do supervisory management. Of course, the cockroach soon has to hire a spider to manage the office, the files and the reports which the cockroach is especially good at writing. But the spider too needs an assistant, and hires a fly. To be seen to be efficient they soon call in an owl as a consultant to help streamline the process. The owl sees the office is now overstaffed, so the Big Lion sacks the ant because its production has gone down steadily over the expansion period. It was too busy filling out forms to do its job.

An all-too-familiar story. There are fewer police on the beat, teachers in the classroom and nurses on the ward because they are all filling out forms. Performance management and appraisal cancer?

There is absolutely no mystery in what a good doctor, manager or teacher is like. Ask anyone, as a simple training exercise, to list the qualities of a good boss and they will have no difficulty. There is also considerable consensus: across cultures, sectors, time periods.

A good boss helps you clarify your goals/targets/key performance indicators (KPIs), but more than that gives you the support you need. A good manager encourages and rewards as well as giving you the tools to do the job. At school it was the teacher, not the subject that made the difference: one could light a fire of enthusiasm as quickly as another could extinguish it.

These good professionals have an instinctive knowledge of what to do and the motivation to do it. And they soon reap considerable rewards. Because, as they say, what goes around, comes around. They don't need training, help, forms and so on.

But that is not the problem. The real problem is the lazy, indolent, incompetent professional. The teacher whose commitment is perfunctory; the GP who is never the patient's choice at the surgery; and the boss whose department shows a remarkable staff turnover.

We have known for nearly 100 years that where output can be reliably and accurately measured (the first study involved the Sheffield Steel Works) the best 10 percent of the workforce produce around 2½ times more than the bottom 10 percent. There is considerable variability in performance. So what to do about poor performers? What about the inadequate or defensive boss who won't ever discuss with their staff how they are doing? The teacher whose pupils always get lower grades than their colleagues'? The store manager whose profits are much below target, expectations and those of other managers?

The answer, of course, is threefold: first, get a good, reliable measure of performance that provides you with the evidence you need; second, institute policies and processes that require managers to do the things that good managers do; and third, ensure the new system works in the sense that all the people at or above a certain level do the same thing.

And this is how it all begins. Finding, recording and logging KPIs. All the paperwork and training to ensure managers carry out progress reviews and annual appraisals in the prescribed way. And, of course, the management police need to check everything is done on time and in the correct way. This takes manpower: computer systems need to be set up, monitored and updated. Managers have to be trained. And consultants may have to be brought in to help with the particularly tricky bits.

We all know exactly what this leads to: behavior recording, form-filling and all that wonderful inventiveness that goes with fudging the data.

The central question is the effect all this has on our good and bad managers. The answer is pure disaster: good managers become angry and alienated because their time and effort is spent on bureaucratic detail. Further, meeting their new targets changes the ways in which they behave, so reducing their efficacy. Demoralized, they seem to lose their focus and take early retirement.

And the bad ones, at whom the whole system is aimed? Do they become better managers? There is an easy way to find out: do a "before and after" of the introduction of the system. Grudgingly, they attend a training course and fill out forms. But, like almost all in the organization, they conspire to find new ways to cheat the system (which is usually not very difficult).

And the result: there is now a huge department instituting a system that alienates the good people and has little effect on the bad people, with the average person becoming cynical about the whole thing. The question is whether it is all worth it? Do performance management systems work?

# Faking it

Some people totally dismiss the idea of using questionnaires in selection, on the grounds that respondents can "fake their answers." Paradoxically, the same people seem quite happy with selection on the basis of an interview, perhaps believing that interviewees couldn't fake in this situation, or that faking would readily be spotted.

So what is faking? Why do people fake? In fact, don't we all fake all the time? And isn't faking a crucial business skill? Rather than *select out* fakers, should you not use it as a crucial *select in* criterion? And most cynical/sceptical of all, is it possible to be yourself and not be a faker in business life ... if you want to be successful?

To fake means to sham, feign or dissimulate. It is a deliberate act of deception. It is the presentation of something or someone that is inauthentic, disingenuous and insincere. We can talk about impression management or telling "porkie pies."

But isn't impression management a very useful social skill? Is it not at the heart of PR? All those books on how to present oneself in interviews are not called "Fakery at an Interview." Presentation skills courses are not called "Faking Commitment."

All service jobs involve social skills and emotional labor. The way an employee speaks, dresses, smiles and so on has to be learned. Some people are better at it than others. They are what psychologists call "high self-monitors." They are concerned with expressive self-presentation. They tend to monitor themselves and their behavior to ensure that they provide an appropriate or desired public appearance. They watch other people for signs of what to do. They are self-conscious and concerned about looking good.

There are three types of faking on questionnaires or at interviews. The *first* is telling deliberate, conscious and serious lies, such as claiming to have degrees and qualifications that the interviewee does not have. Then there are sins of omission and commission: "forgetting" or not admitting crucial and asked-for information such as criminal convictions or bankruptcy. Or telling serious fibs about previous employment, for how long and at what salary.

The issue is, what is serious and what is not. This takes one into the subtle issues of "white lies" and so on. But most people don't have many problems when thinking about what is a serious business-oriented lie. This is quite different from mastering presentation skills, putting your best foot forward, or acting appropriately.

The *second* form of faking is perhaps more serious. It is, in essence, being deluded. In this case, people supposedly consciously have beliefs about their abilities, motivation, looks and so on which objectively, or at least as observed by all who know them, are patently untrue. Thus there is the narcissistic egocentric who claims to be a caring person, a good listener or a thoughtful friend. Or the "jobsworths" who apparently believe they have good customer service skills. They are really faking, but not consciously so.

The *third* type of faking is the sort we have been trained to do since childhood. We mind our Ps and Qs; we don't say things (we might believe) that can hurt or insult people; we dress for the occasion and so on. It is called obeying social etiquette. And there is an etiquette for interviews. Both interviewer and interviewees have specific roles to play.

So what of the person who can't or doesn't do impression-management-type fakery at the interview? Are they scrupulously honest, low self-monitors praised for presenting themselves as they really are? Or are they naïve, socially unskilled people unlikely to succeed in any service job?

The idea of *emotional labor* is that workers are expected to display specific emotions at work to promote organizational goals. It involves employees displaying and regulating their emotions constantly so they are consistent with "display rules" at work, whether or not they represent the employees' actual feelings. It's not a choice: it is a work requirement.

Is it going too far to suggest that no successful person can be totally themselves at work? Could you really let it all hang out, say and show what you think and feel? Of course not. Employees have to be diplomatic, tactful and subtle. Sir Henry Wotton, an English author and diplomat who was the ambassador to Venice in the seventeenth century, observed that "An ambassador is a man of virtue sent abroad to lie for his country while a news writer is a man without virtue who lies at home for himself." He also said "Tell the truth, and so puzzle and confound your adversaries."

So do tact, diplomacy and charm comprise a form of faking? It depends on one's definition, but certainly it's a skill. Of course, in unguarded moments, or when one is "backstage" it may be possible to get a glimpse of the real character in front of you. Some people reserve their authentic feelings for when they are at home or with fellow workmates in the canteen. It is difficult to fake for long periods of time in different tasks or within institutions with different demands.

One conclusion of all this, of course, is that rather than dislike, dismiss or demean the faker at work, they should be rewarded and selected. They know how to behave on the job.

# Face-ism and shape-ism at work

Do physically attractive people have an advantage at work? Are they more likely to be selected, promoted and better paid than their unfortunately less attractive colleagues? Does attractiveness count more than being competent? Is the issue of the occupational and economic consequences of physical attractiveness more significant for women than for men? And if there is face-ism, shape-ism and body-ism at work, should we try to do something about it? Isn't it all so unfair?

Yet all of us know a beautiful or handsome person who is clinically unable, it seems, to accept the fact. More often females than males, poorly adjusted and emotionally unstable, many through their demeanor succeed in proving the point.

Perceived or self-rated physical attractiveness gives people greater confidence in their other abilities. It raises expectations. There is evidence that they ask for more, go for better jobs, and soon earn more than others.

Studies have yet to be done on that most unusual of outliers, the physically unattractive person who thinks they are attractive – a view not shared by others. This would be the real test for hypotheses that self-rated attractiveness is a more powerful determinant of other people's behavior than "other-rated" good looks.

There is plenty of evidence of the effect of various physical characteristics:

*Hair color*: blondes are paid more and are more effective at eliciting donations than brunettes of equal attractiveness.

*Weight:* waist circumference is negatively associated with wages for women, but not for men. All measures of obesity (such as body mass index – BMI) are negatively associated with many employment factors (selection, salary) and strongly related to reported discrimination.

*Height*: height is related to pay and promotability.

*Facial attractiveness*: this predicts higher starting and later work salaries. It is also consistently related to perceived competence and hireability.

There are numerous other studies that have focused on very specific body features such hip-to-waist ratio, physical deformities, even tattoos and the impressions others have of them. Some research suggests physical attractiveness can have very different effects in same sex versus opposite sex interviewers. Highly attractive people are less likely than moderately attractive people to be hired, particularly if the same-sex hirers are themselves only moderately attractive.

But the "pretty is good: handsome is talented" literature has three problems. The *first* is that the findings are not always consistent. The evidence is equivocal: some studies don't confirm the findings of others. *Second*, this research is fairly difficult because so many features have to be studied. It's not just a matter of interviewing blondes and brunettes: all other physical aspects of the individuals as well as their language, voice and dress have to be similar. Often such a study has to be done using actors in different coloured wigs or with dyed hair.

The *third* is the major problem. It's called interaction effects. Studies that have wisely investigated these have shown how complicated the whole thing is. So take any one characteristic, say height: taller people do better at work. This may be true for men and but not for women. It may also not be a linear relationship. There is an optimal height – say, 6′2″ to 6′4″ – but being 6′8″ makes you a freak. Perhaps very tall women are significantly disadvantaged. And then it may depend on the nature of the job. Height may be important in business but not in teaching, say.

More important, there is the thorny issue of co-variation. To do the studies properly you need to keep all the other factors constant while comparing the individuals on the one criterion. So if you want to see if body shape affects promotability you need people of varying body shapes but similar height, hair color, facial attractiveness and so on. But what if these factors are confounded: that weight affects shape of face, skin clarity and so on? Difficult to untangle all of this.

When it comes to what should be done we have the vulgar evolutionary theorists against the ignorant social policy interventionists. Some evolutionary psychologists have argued that there is clear evidence that attractiveness is a real marker of other traits such as intelligence. As mating opportunities and strategies – that is, rich men have more attractive mates than poor men – there are in life physical indicators of psychological characteristics. Thus, to some extent, "What is beautiful is good"; Amen.

The logic of some evolutionary psychology is simple: more intelligent men achieve higher status (wealth, power, rank) than less intelligent men; high status men have more choice of beautiful women; intelligence and beauty are heritable; QED – beauty is linked to brains. Though this logic is debated, the taste for sociobiology in, for example, the popular Mars/ Venus book (Gray, 2004) makes these ideas acceptable to many.

But what if you think something needs to be done? It is bad enough being plain, but worse being discriminated against in life settings. So take photographs off application forms. Make sure interviewers are of both sexes. Make it all much more evidence-based.

We know the more structured and competency based the interview, the less these "superficial" factors play a part. Attractiveness encourages the halo effect – the idea that suggests all other features of an individual are also attractive.

So don't go down the insensitive, backfiring, anti-business legislative route. Just learn to be a bit more structured and evidence-based. And if the top people are eventually somewhat more attractive than those at the bottom, then so be it.

## Reference

Gray, J. (2004) *Men are from Mars, Women are from Venus.* New York; HarperCollins.

# Food at work

School dinners are a political, educational and dietary "hot potato." Should they be free for all pupils, or should some pay? What should or should not be on the menu? Are school meals about health education? Should schools ban fizzy drinks? Or chips? What role should schools play in dietary literacy? And what of the religious minefield that food represents? Worse, what of galloping allergies and the shadow of compensation lawyers who are eager to sue the organization for not serving nut-free num-nums at a Christmas party? All too hot to handle? Let the little darlings bring their own food.

Food at work seems a much less contentious issue. Some organizations have canteens; some only a few machines, and many leave people to fend for themselves. Some develop a cosy relationship with a restaurant chain. That is, within the building, beyond the guard posts, there is a small, franchised restaurant selling a limited number of items that the company has learned are popular with its employees. Normal prices, but just very convenient.

The statistics around people grabbing a sandwich at lunchtime are surprising. Most people, it seems, multi-task around food. They eat and email at the same time. Crumbs clog keyboards. People do cold food, fast food, old food. And they do it quickly – the very opposite of the French approach.

Does it matter? Does food really have an impact on performance? And if it does, what should organizations do about it? What of the busy knowledge worker who arrives at work having downed two soft drinks at the station and who keeps going on a chocolate bar till they're free to grab a quick sandwich at lunchtime? Is mood or cognitive performance affected in these circumstances?

The answer to this question depends on whom you ask. Speak to security experts and we are all under threat; speak to counsellors and we are all stressed; speak to health and safety people and we are all massively accident prone. And speak to health experts and they all testify to the importance of the quality and quantity of food people eat.

There are *three* aspects of food that are important at work: cognitive and physical performance; social effects; and mood effects.

## Cognitive and physical performance

Food is fuel. Human beings need it in order to perform efficiently. People starved of food and water for whatever reason make mistakes, are slower and less efficient. Studies by nutritionists have shown the relatively quick and powerful effects of various types of food on performance. Lack of food or poor-quality food can be demoralizing.

We are told that "an army marches on its stomach." And we know that hungry people make less good decisions. Restaurants usually encourage their staff to eat before serving their guests. This is important for portion control and to maintain energy levels during difficult periods. One well-known construction business became famous because the founder had the belief that his men worked harder and better after a good breakfast. Thus the day began by each worker being given a free hearty breakfast, which helped manual laborers to do their best work early in the day. Some tasks require stamina; others concentration.

### Social effects

Human beings are social animals. We know the symbolic power of the family meal, the Last Supper, the gala dinner. We celebrate with food. Feasts are held at weddings, and sometimes funerals. We chat, mingle and relax. One supermarket chain tried to determine what factors related best to the morale of the organization as a whole. It turned out to be the canteen: size, comfort, private zones, quality and quantity of hot food.

People meet over food. The days are gone of the executive dining room. Wise managers use lunch as an opportunity to mingle with their staff; to test the temperature under amiable conditions. Contact is made in non-threatening circumstances.

### Mood effects

Mood influences behavior in powerful but subtle ways, and all retailers know this. They use aromas to make customers feel, say, "Christmassy". The smell of coconut shampoo puts people in a carefree holiday mood. People trying to sell houses use fresh flowers or get the smell of good coffee wafting through the house. Better still, give the potential buyers a hot drink and they will feel warmer about the house. Music also affects mood. It can affect the speed at which people do things. Again, music often has significant event markers attached to it.

Observe people before, during and after lunch. Their mood changes, often from irritated to relaxed, frenetic to chilled. Mood has an impact on others and that is why it is important.

But it is diet rather than individual meals that has the real impact: diets don't work, but lifestyle changes do. There is no such thing as junk food, only the way people eat a balanced diet or not. Personal diet is a function of many things – religion, education, culture – but most often is a result of habit and availability. Organizations can play an important part in this. At the time of writing, the government is trying to "nudge" rather than dictate. They might consider tax relief for organizations that provide sub-sidized good food to eat on the premises. Good for the organization and good for the government itself in the long run.

# Gender and job satisfaction

Most of us have heard of the glass ceiling. But what of the glass cliff, the glass escalator or the sticky floor? All are "cute" metaphors for the fact that women seem to be discriminated against at work.

There are far fewer women CEOs, on boards or starting their own companies than men. Every so often we are given the shock statistics and told something must be done to end this appalling situation. It's not only unfair but makes no business sense.

Reactions to the issue vary from legislative to turning a blind eye. The equality-sensitive Scandinavians have demanded that companies above a certain size have a 50:50 ratio of women to men on the board. Others "tut-tut" and talk of tokenism, quota-madness and the whole enterprise backfiring. Wags maintain that women are clever enough not to want to trade off sanity and happiness for the madness and trinkets of the top-team life style.

The arguments for gender equality of opportunity are compelling from both a moral and an economic standpoint. Like so many areas of change, once it has been carried out one wonders why it did not happen earlier: smoking in public areas, women priests, seat belt legislation and so on. There are, of course, exceptions just as easy to mention, generally a matter of personal taste, though health and safety legislation springs to mind.

But for the social science researchers in this area there remains an interesting paradox. Why is it that so many studies, looking at many different groups (doctors, lawyers, oil-rig workers, police) in different countries (on all continents) show that, overall, women's job satisfaction is not (significantly) lower than men's, given their obvious and acknowledged disadvantages with regard to autonomy, pay and promotion opportunities. While, inevitably, some studies do show sex differences in both directions, with some showing men and others women having greater job satisfaction, the vast majority show no overall difference. The question is, why?

There are three standard answers to this conundrum. *First*, women have, overall, lower expectations than men, partly because they compare themselves with other women. They expect less, get less, but are also satisfied with less. It's the social comparison argument. Women are still portrayed as exclusively concerned with child care and domestic work. Watch the news, read the papers, read the annual reports. It's all chaps. Yes, there are exceptions, and increasingly more of them. But until the number of role models increase, and until it becomes normal for women to reach high positions, they will be "content" to stay at lower levels, like everyone else in their cohort.

This explanation means that unless one follows the Scandinavian model of forcing, demanding and legally enshrining gender equality, it will never happen.

The *second* explanation is that women are socialized not to express discontent, rage or dissent. That may be true of some cultures more than others. This is all part of the socialization into acceptance (of one's fate) but also of humility. Boys do hubris (arrogance, power-play, ambition), girls do humility. Men lead and decide, women care and share. So perhaps women are really not as job-satisfied as men but simply don't say so. Not porkie-pies, self-deception, or impression-management. Just "obeying" the injunctions of the culture instilled so rigorously.

Again, this may be changing. Women now seem happier to complain and to go on strike. It was said that men did "industrial action" and women went absent when dissatisfied. Even if that were true, it does seem to be changing now.

The *third* explanation is that women and men value quite different aspects of a job. Women place more value on intrinsic rewards such as relationships with supervisors and co-workers, and the "psychological" working conditions alongside the nature of the work itself. Men, on the other hand, rate more highly the extrinsic factors such as pay, promotion, prospects and company prestige.

Thus, it is argued that, if the intrinsic conditions are right, then lower-paid women with fewer opportunities express as much job satisfaction as more highly paid, more senior men in the organization. The women get what they want, the men get what they want, and everybody is happy.

This partly explains why the sexes are differentially attracted to a range of jobs. Men are prepared to put up with less interesting, more stressful, less autonomous work for more money, while women will trade off the salary, benefits and power-thing for happiness at work. This explanation does make sense. And it can, in part, account for the equivocal findings from previous studies on job satisfaction differences between the sexes.

It has also been suggested that men and women who do MBAs have different aims: clever women are often there to find a husband with excellent earning power.

But two questions remain. First, what other factors/explanations play a part? What about the role of personality or ability? Surely if the job-fit is wrong there will be dissatisfaction. And if there are well-established sex differences in personality and ability, will this not have some impact?

And second, where do these different values come from in the first place? Why are men so obsessed with the Ps – pay, promotion and power? Here, if you like, we can turn to socio-biology. But that's another story.

# Gossip is good for you

No want likes to be thought of as "a gossip": a spreader of "tittle-tattle"; a malicious rumor monger; a time-wasting sniper at the great and the good. But we love gossip; and it sells. Whole magazines are dedicated to it. It is the life-blood of the best water-cooler moments. Nothing like a bit of juicy gossip about some cold, supercilious, senior manager.

From where does the pervasiveness and function of gossip come? The word "gossip" is derived from the concept of a crony or kinsman. It is the chatty talk of peers, the in-group. Gossip can be positive or negative, but to "scandal about someone" is exclusively negative. It is to bring into disrepute, to defame or to disgrace others, and it seems to spread most in uncertain and unhappy times.

Gossip is much more than "small talk." Its function is usually more than simple entertainment, or revenge. Gossips spread rumors about people, plans and processes. Rumors have been known to cause panic and riots. "Idle gossip", as the population was told in the war, "costs lives."

But clever marketers love gossip: it's called word-of-mouth marketing. It's cheap, very efficient and can ensure "tipping points." In fact, many advertisements portray people as gossiping about amazing, new wonderful products they have found.

So what is office gossip usually about? The same topics appear again and again. The control of resources, usually money, but often space and information flow. Gossip is about what really happens at work, not what the PR people want employees to think. And there is as always gossip about "Ugandan affairs," rumpy-pumpy at the office party, sexual activity of all kinds. Third, gossip about power and relationships, such as alliances and political dealings between interested parties.

There are gossip enthusiasts: some who transmit, others who receive. But what is its social function? Why has it, and does it, occur in all groups at all times? First, gossip is there

- To remind group members of the group's real and important values and acceptable norms of behavior. It is often about those who break the rules.
- To act as an effective deterrent to deviance. It tells of the "comeuppance" of those who thought they were beyond reproof.

- To punish those who transgress the norms. Gossip destroys reputations and therefore futures.

Gossip has been described as order without law: the way that neighbors settle disputes. Notice how much of the script of soap operas is about gossip. Gossip can be about indirect aggression and about establishing and strengthening sanctions.

So gossip is about uncovering cheats. It is also a levelling mechanism used to neutralize those who get above their station or attempt to compromise the interests of the group. Gossip, along with ridicule and ostracism, is used among various groups to keep control. Gossip flourishes in the playground and the canteen as much as in the pub. It is also used by Machiavellian individuals in attempts to further their own ends.

People find gossip more interesting if it is (a) negative (scandals, misfortunes, misjudgement); or (b) about high- (rather than low-) status people. People spread positive gossip about allies (such as about promotions) but negative information about enemies.

Those with whom we prefer to share gossip tend to be people of the same sex, of a similar age and at a similar level at work. People gather in groups and enjoy a good gossip about the bosses, the customers and the shareholders they dislike. Nothing like a bit of tittle-tattle about sexual infidelity or dysfunction, promiscuity, drunken behavior or drug/gambling/other addictions, or even major or minor theft.

So, can gossip be positive? That is, can it involve how clever, talented, motivated or honest a person is? In this, can gossip serve its many functions by creating ideal models. That doesn't sound right. That sounds like PR, which is the very opposite of gossip. *Hello!* magazine seems to be the epitome of positive gossip. Positive gossip is about private lives: about the little, often trivial, things that people do that remain confidential: food preferences, curious habits and so on.

Gossip is nearly always publicly denounced, but frequently socially valued. If you look at attitudes to gossips and gossiping, there seem two clear factors. The first stresses the social value of gossip as a way of sharing information about others. When is a gossip a whistle-blower? There is also a moral factor, which asks the difficult question about the truthfulness of gossip and the underhand way in which it occurs. Informers can be seen as gossips.

Does gossip change much over the life-span? Who gossips most – men or women? When do children first begin to gossip? And what about? It's a very interesting topic, but is it worthy of research?

Certainly, gossipping happens at work. Study a rumor and you'll find a social network – people in the know. Rename gossip information-communication and you see why it is really important. That is why organizations wisely, but not always successfully, try to subvert gossipy rumors by press releases and internal communications of one sort of another.

But you can't legislate against it or control it. Indeed, attempts to control it would probably backfire – and become a topic of very juicy gossip.

# Hating HR

In 2005, the deputy editor, Keith Hammonds, of *Fast Company* magazine wrote an article called "Why We Hate HR" (2005) that is still quoted extensively. And, curiously, it is the more courageous members of the HR community who quote it the most.

Hammonds began by arguing that HR had proved "at best a necessary evil – and at worst, a dark bureaucratic force that blindly enforces nonsensical rules, resists creativity and impedes constructive change."

He makes the usual complaints: appraisals are too often simultaneously massively time-consuming and useless. HR people stress the importance of communication but their output is full of gobbledegook and flouts reality. Many are just henchmen of the chief financial officer (CFO) in their endeavor to cut benefits and reduce the payroll. And their processes are duplicative, wasteful and pointless.

Hammonds noted that the things HR are usually good at – the administration of pay, benefits, retirement – are being outsourced, with most HR departments ghettoizing themselves on the brink of extinction. Administration is easy and cheap to do, so economic natural selection leads to outsourcing or the downsizing of the department.

He offers four explanations for the universal dislike, disrespect and disparagement of HR:

1. They aren't bright enough. Or in his jolly American terminology, they "aren't the sharpest tacks in the box"; "HR represents a relatively low risk parking spot"; "they aren't particularly interested in, or equipped for, doing business." They can't answer questions such as who is the organizations's core customer or the company's most important competitor. And they neither understand nor are interested in finance, which ultimately marginalizes them.
2. HR pursues efficiency over value because it is easy to measure. It's not a case of X percent of people attending Y percent of training programmes, or Z percent of appraisals being correctly completed on time, but rather what real value all this add for all the stakeholders, particularly investors and customers. Few HR metrics are linked to business performance. The implication is that they should be, and if they can't demonstrate value they should be dropped.

3. Most people say HR does not work for them. Paradoxically, Hammonds notes that HR pursues process and procedural standardization and uniformity in the face of an increasingly complex, diverse workforce. One-size-fits-all is easier and is claimed to be fairer. An obsession with equality over equity means the vital lesson is forgotten that the company most values and rewards high-performing employees. HR shoot a good line about excellence and top performance, but rarely reward it.

4. HR people rarely make it to the top. They don't get the corner office, and they don't get the ear of top management. One reason is a lack of strategic planning. HR focuses on training and development and if you are lucky, improving bottom-line performance, but rarely does the big picture.

The message of Hammonds' article is that HR will only be useful and liked if it understands the business: profit-and-loss (P&L) sensibility and competitor analysis strategy. That is why people who move from line to HR positions are often best at the job. They do understand the business.

HR takes a great "change" line but often finds it difficult to keep up because strategy moves too fast. Further, the strategy may be somewhat whimsical, based on the caprice of a powerful leader or board, which makes it difficult to implement necessary changes.

The questions, class, are these: First, was this analysis essentially correct or not? Second, is it in full, or in part, still true today? And third, what advice would you give to a CEO about what to do with the HR section?

Has "HR bashing" become a new sport? Is it a vicious, nasty attack on the most defenceless part of the organization? Does it have, at least in part, therapeutic value? In fact, HR people are among the most self-critical of all departments. You rarely see the finance, engineering or marketing departments doing the soul-searching self-criticism done by HR. But perhaps for HR it is really little more than a mantra or even a talisman. It can't be much fun being in HR, which may explain why they often change their title to the "People Department" or the "Talent Management Team."

So what is your advice to the CEO? Insist that all HR professionals have significant line management experience? Insist that there is evidence of the value-added for all that bureaucratic stuff? Change reporting lines?

Certainly, governments filled with lawyers have had a field day with new employment laws. From paternity leave to ever crazier health and safety regulations, it has become a complex technical field. HR people often have to take the flak for trying to apply government regulations that make it much harder to do business.

HR people tend to be very cautious, reactive rather than proactive, which partly explains their lack of interest in strategy. The problem lies to some extent in their training and outlook.

So some radical suggestions for the CEO. Never hire a senior HR person who has not had significant line experience, or even better, shown evidence of entrepreneurial behavior. Insist that all metrics and processes are linked to bottom-line performance. Worry most about payroll and compliance. Keep the ratio low.

## Reference

Hammonds, K. (2005) "Why We Hate HR," *Fast Company*, August.

# How management style leads directly to profit and loss

The service profit chain "theory" first published as a *Harvard Business School Review* paper and later as a successful book (Heskett *et al*. 1994), was based on a causal chain model which led from employee satisfaction to profit.

It showed a causal path that went like this: internal service quality (processes, procedures and management style) related directly to employee satisfaction, which drove both retention and productivity. These, in turn, drove the value proposition or the service concept for customers, and this led to customer loyalty, which influenced both revenue growth and profitability.

On the extreme left was the ultimate goal: profit. This was, in the service business, a function of repeat business by happy customers. It was the excellent (don't just satisfy me, delight me) service that did the trick. And this in turn was driven by good managers, a healthy adaptive culture and good management practices. Good managers chose and motivated good staff who consistently delivered the golden eggs. And management style is determined primarily by the managers' ability, personality and values.

There are some crucial concepts in this model for sustained profitability.

### Customer loyalty and satisfaction

Companies with profit and growth are characterized by a large number of loyal repeat customers who seek out the specific product and services of the company. Loyal customers are more likely to tell others about their loyalty than "just" satisfied customers. Customer loyalty is driven by employees. Managers often have little direct contact with customers but their direct influence on employees is very significant.

They have to cultivate a productive employee, but shape and develop a cohesive team of individuals who share a passion for the business. Some customers defect from organizations, others are indifferent; some are even affectionate. It is only the latter that are really loyal. A satisfied customer is not automatically a loyal customer unless they have no choice. It is only the highly satisfied customers who become loyal. Customer expectations change all the time. If a company wants to maintain customers' loyalty it has to continually get better and outperform its rivals.

### Value

Satisfaction depends on the company's ability to create value for the customer. Value means that the customer has gained *more* from the product than he or she thinks it is worth. Value often has an *emotional* aspect that makes an experience particularly memorable for the customer. The key to creating value is the ability to *bond emotionally*. Value is created by loyal employees.

### Employee productivity

Satisfied and loyal employees are far more productive. Value is related to the employee's ability to act on the wishes and needs of the customers and find solutions. Productive employees usually have a higher degree of product and customer knowledge. Thus employees who have served a number of years in the company are usually much more productive than new employees.

### Employee loyalty

Employee loyalty is driven by enthusiasm and satisfaction: engagement and commitment. To be able to create excited customers and contribute to memorable experiences employees also need to be excited. This implies that the employees must be happy with their jobs to be able to meet the customers' complex and immediate needs. Loyalty refers to considerate employees who stay a long time in the company and have an extensive knowledge of customers, processes and the culture within the company.

### Employee satisfaction

Employee loyalty is driven by employee satisfaction. Just as customer loyalty is driven by engagement rather than satisfaction alone, employee loyalty depends on the same principle. Employee "satisfaction" is not the same as engagement, which is more difficult and much more complex. In the service profit chain, employee satisfaction is a result of "internal quality," which again relates to a number of elements that have to be present to ensure employee satisfaction.

## Managerial style

Managers lead as a function of their ability, personality and values. These usually determine the sort of experience managers have had before, during and outside work. A good manager is able to inspire, engage and motivate his or her staff as quickly and as thoroughly as a bad one can do the opposite. Even if the systems in place and the product are not ideal, good managers can still get the very best out of their staff.

It is important to recognize that leadership and management style underly the chain's success. Individual managers motivate and reward; they create and sustain a healthy, productive culture. Thus the questions for leaders are: do all employees know who their customers are? And perhaps more important, are they satisfied with the technical and personal support and direction they receive in their job? The more the leadership is energetic, participatory, caring, listening and coaching-oriented versus elitist, detached and supervisory, the better. And what determines the way that a person undertakes management is his/her personality, ability and values, as noted above.

Exit interviews demonstrate that people don't resign from jobs as such; they resign because of individual managers. And appraisal interviews show that people stay engaged and productive because of individual managers. That is why managerial selection and promotion are so important.

## Reference

Heskett, J.L., Jones, T.O., Loveman, G.W., Sasser, W.E. and Schelsinger, L.A. (1994) "Putting the Service Profit Chain to Work," *Harvard Business Review*, March–April: 164–74.

# The hyper-moral obsessive

Certain jobs attract certain types, sometimes pathological types. Paranoid types may be attracted to the security sector, and narcissists to politics and show business. Vocational choice is determined by one's temperament and character, as well as personal values.

However, the job one ends up in is a function of other things as well, such as education, parenting style and sheer chance.

There are many jobs that suit the obsessive-compulsive personality: quality control, internal audit, health and safety. Of course, there are degrees of obsessive compulsiveness. At the extreme it can be manifested as a severe psychiatric personality disorder characterized by intrusive worries and repetitive thoughts, and revealed by ritualized behavioral or mental acts aimed at neutralizing the obsessive thoughts.

Obsessive compulsiveness (OC) may be characterized by constant washing and fear of dirt, by hoarding valueless objects, or the constant writing of ordered lists. Compulsives are constantly checking things which may help them at work. They like certainty. They talk about "getting it right" and like rules, processes and procedures which do just that. They believe in all sorts of control, particularly the control of thoughts and passions. Many believe that their own thoughts have the power to cause or influence every situation and action.

Most people know a mildly OC person. They may be labelled "anal obsessive" in Freudian terminology. They often lead very orderly lives. They follow rituals. Their possessions are neat, ordered and super-tidy. They can have extraordinary little quirks such as color-coding their clothes, arranging groceries by country of origin or by shape of container or calorific content. They may have a reputation for being perfectionists or creators of "to-do" lists.

But when their rituals are threatened or curtailed they can become very nasty. Have you ever challenged a quality controller or a health and safety killjoy? Many start with a passive-aggressive response, but this can quickly change to something more direct.

There used to be a distinction in the psychiatric literature between two distinct types of personality disorder, though there is often a good deal of co-morbidity, meaning that people can have both at the same time. One disorder was labelled passive-aggressive, the other obsessive-compulsive.

But passive-aggressiveness – a leisurely ignoring of others' requests and becoming cross when asked to do things – is so common that it is now no longer considered pathological and has been removed from the list of psychiatric disorders.

Sigmund Freud wrote some notes on one of his "cases" who suffered from a obsessive-compulsive disorder (OCD). He noted that those with OCD had feelings of extreme or hyper-morality. All analysts argue that aggression or hostility toward (specific) other people are often not openly expressed but manifest in fantasies or more often in an unconscious form.

Freud's idea was that obsessionals are uber-moralists as a result of a defence mechanism called "reaction formation" against latent aggressive impulses. Reaction formation is a primitive coping strategy that attempts to calm and eradicate socially unacceptable impulses or wishes by out-wardly adopting the opposite impulse or behavior. So the OCD person becomes very moral and over-responsible, to try to cope with these barely understood thoughts.

However, for most people the strategy is only partly successful, and all those aggressive blasphemies and sexual impulses return. But these are what the psychobabblers call "ego-alien" because they are not part of the self-concept of the moral OCD person.

So, the theory goes, many OCD people are stuck in an ambivalent attitude to many other people. Their inflated responsibility-taking is not in truth a real concern for the well-being of others, but rather an overcompensation for aggressive and calculating reciprocal behavior.

But the theory does not say whether latent aggression precedes, accompanies or follows OCD. So do OCD people develop a hatred of people who won't comply with their strange demands? Family members who resist taking part in curious rituals can become targets of anger and resentment, even violence, which forms a vicious circle. They feel guilty with self-blame and are over-compensatorily penitent. This dichotomy may account for the higher incidence of suicide among OCD people.

Psychiatrists interested in this phenomenon try to help OCD patients by normalizing the fact that aggression and hostility toward others is common. It does not mean one is a bad person or that one is at risk of actually being hostile or violent. They are then taught how to express negative emotions assertively and in a mature, socially competent way. It's all about trying to resist the suppression of these thoughts and obsessive rumination.

All very interesting, but what has this got to do with work? The answer lies in the mildly OCD auditors, quality controllers or health and safety experts who cross the line. Many put on a "holier-than-thou," self-righteous act. Indeed, they are rewarded for this: for being incorruptible, highly moral people.

But the anger does manifest itself when challenged. Try having an "evidence-based" conversation with someone who is insisting on the introduction of some pointless, bureaucratic activity. Try pointing out the law of unintended consequences where safety procedures paradoxically put one more at risk. Try suggesting that their procedures fundamentally undermine the long-term profitability and survival of the organization. Then you see the latent aggression becoming rather more manifest.

# Improving references

Most references are a complete waste of time, both for those who write them and those who seek them. They provide little or misleading information and, as such, often lead to poor people decisions. In fact they may significantly add to decision error in selection rather than improve it.

The laziest (and a very common) approach is to send a previous employer a badly photocopied, gobbledegook job description and a request to complete a few open-ended sentences, disclose absenteeism statistics (if they are in the public sector) or tick a few boxes. The sender never checks how much the referee knows about the employee or the nature of their relationship. Names are usually supplied by the candidate in the hope that those they nominate will impress or write "good things" about them.

An increasing number of organizations forbid the writing of references. They know references just feed avaricious lawyers. You can be taken to court if you write a good reference for a poor employee (relieved to see them go) or bad references for employees who have convinced themselves (despite any real evidence) that they are star performers. But the lawyers have a trick up their sleeve: if you fail to write a reference knowing that somebody had a criminal record, was a sexual harasser or child molester, you are still taken to court. Damned if you do; damned if you don't.

References can, in principle, be very valuable indeed. People do clever impression management at interviews and on questionnaires. It might be difficult to get behind the mask. Some don't really fake but they are deluded about their attributes, work ethic and productivity. References should solve the faking problem. Better still if the organization has got good records of the employee's behavior at work – though this is very rare indeed. Most people's files contain precious little of use except a few fudged appraisal forms. Organizations are surprisingly amnesic about staff performance details.

References are only useful if three criteria are met. *First*, that the right people are asked to give them. This means those in the know. It is often the bosses who are asked to write the references. But what do they know? What do colleagues, reports and customers know? Subordinates always know more than bosses. They know about management style, and foibles, preferences and peccadilloes. They usually have ten times as much contact as bosses. Colleagues (peers) know about abilities and ambitions.

Customers know about keeping promises. This is why multi-source (360°) feedback and ratings are so interesting.

Lecturers are often asked to write references for students they taught 10 years previously in classes of over 100. And, in many universities, lectures are voluntary. So first establish how well the referees know the candidate. In what context (at work; out of work) and for how long? What was the nature of their relationship? In short, what is their data bank? The more they know about all aspects of the person (personality, ability, work style, values) the better.

*Second*, are they prepared to tell you the truth? Are they prepared to talk/write? For many there is little or no incentive to do so. And if there is indeed an incentive (to help get rid of a poor worker; help a relative; knife a talented colleague; get revenge on a person) it may be seriously counterproductive. Referees, quite rightly, are nervous about writing references that can later turn out to be Exhibit A. So why not speak to them. It is less effort for the referee and, given that they are not being recorded, probably leads to much more disclosure. They should be encouraged to say "I don't know" if indeed they don't. And they may be asked to state how confident they are in their answers and/or their source(s) of information.

*Third*, ask direct, specific questions regarding behaviors and values you want to know about. And be clear what you want to know, and why. So if you want to know about abilities, ask about speed and accuracy; the quality of written work; capacity for learning; and the candidate's general knowledge. If you want to (and you should) know about a personal work ethic, ask about qualities such as striving for achievement and being well organized. How well prepared for important meetings/presentations? And does the candidate have a reputation for hard work? Ask about coping with stress; about illnesses, absenteeism, moodiness.

If people are asked to rate somebody after a free response it is still possible to ask 20–30 significant questions and get the answers in 15 minutes. But it is important that you are clear about what you want to know, and why.

Telephone interviews are cheap and efficient. But it takes a lot more preparation on the part of the interviewer. You need to find (pinpoint/ target) people who have the information you want, and discover whether they are able to disclose it. Second, the referees need to feel confident about talking to you confidentially. But, perhaps most important, as noted above, you need to know what you want to know, and why, before you start the whole process.

# Incentive schemes

Most employees have the capacity to improve their work-performance and output. Possibly even to double it. And that can significantly increase the sustainability and profitability of the organization. So how to achieve it?

Clearly, employers could pay people more, but that is expensive and doesn't deal with the problem of inefficient work practices. This is equally true of employee benefits such as life assurance, pensions and private health care.

So what are we left with? Non-cash rewards, such as certificates and trophies? Or cheaper one-offs related to performance targets, such as restaurant or store vouchers or an exotic holiday.

Many industries use incentive schemes, particularly those in sectors associated with volume sales (such as automotive, financial services, pharmaceuticals). It's easiest to measure performance in sales because it's simpler to measure items sold, objectively and quantitatively.

The aims of incentive schemes may be manifold. They may be about absenteeism, retention or time-keeping; about teamwork, co-operation or communication. But more often they are about money: reducing costs or increasing productivity.

However, there are many questions to be asked of any scheme initiative on the part of management. Is it about hitting targets (regardless of the number of people who do so) or the top ten (regardless of performance level). Should they commit to targets beforehand (bid-and-make), or see how it goes? Should winners be chosen by lottery, raffle or sweepstake? Should the system be weighted in favor of (or against) specific job titles so that it appears fairer? How should rewards be split up when given to teams (equally, equitably, by rank)? How long should the incentive programme last? Can it be kept simple enough that staff understand how it works and is seen to be fair?

Ask people for their preferred productivity incentive and money (cash) always comes top. But cash is expensive and has little or no trophy value. It's easy, but pretty ineffective as an incentive for those on good salaries. It can also suggest the company is lazy, even cynical.

So what about other things? The latest mobile phone or home computer, perhaps? Company car, private fuel allowance? Or school fee, child care, elderly parent support costs? Membership of a sports or social club?

Of course, the value to the employee of these flexible benefits depends on his/her age and stage. A single man of 25 is very different from a married woman with 3 children under 5 years old, or a single breadwinner in his/her late fifties. So why not offer flexible benefits that are valued equivalently? This could lead to an administrative nightmare soaking up overheads. But the bigger the organization, and the more diverse the workforce, the more complex the issues become.

If the chosen scheme is perceived to be fair and understandable, and the incentives are desirable, management is in with a chance. But incentives often fail because they don't offer what enough people really want, or they are not seen to be fair. Some are so complex that few can understand how they work.

And the favorite incentives? Holidays and travel come pretty near the top. A weekend in Paris; a visit to Disneyland; a shopping expedition to Hong Kong or Singapore. Very desirable, and often surprisingly cheap out of season. One important issue is to get some good internal (and perhaps external) PR for the winner. Two other tricks – first, get the family involved and they'll be able to put pressure on the worker. Second, ensure that the memory lasts (video, photo), by putting the details in the in-house magazine, for example.

Merchandise can be attractive, though it seems a tad old-fashioned now. Could be a reminder of the old Co-op stamps in Britain. But vouchers can work well if they buy things people really need and want, such as clothes, hotel rooms, restaurant meals or gasoline.

The reward of going to some specific event may work: conferences or staff parties, though these can sometimes seem as much like chores as incentives. Remember the joke about the first prize being a week in a Bulgarian resort and the second prize two weeks in the same resort?

And, finally, there are certificates, trophies, letters or exclusive "employee" club membership. But don't underestimate them. After all, what is an MBE, or even a knighthood? Or an invitation to the Queen's garden party? Of course, mementoes can be tacky, soppy or trivial, but in some cultures they are worth everything. Most people wrestle with self-esteem problems and these little things help.

All too complicated? The game not worth the candle? But what are the alternatives? The bottom line is that people can and will work harder and smarter if they want to, and they will if they see the benefits of doing so. And money alone is an unsubtle and insufficient reward.

But there is an elongating and darkening shadow over the staff incentives business. It is, of course, government eager both to tax and to reduce what they see as corruption. The hospitality business, closely linked to the incentive business, has been hit by what many believe to be unjust, insensitive and backfiring legislation.

So, to work out incentives, you need accountants, psychologists and managers. But most important of all these days: you need a lawyer.

# Inspirational teachers

Teachers and trainers can, and do, change lives. They can determine the choice of university and the courses taken. They can have a direct influence on career choices. They can light candles in the darkest mind. They model attitudes, beliefs and behaviors, thereby setting an example to follow. Most important, they can often help people find out what they are good at, passionate about and the things they do in a state of "flow". In short, they help people find their strengths.

Practically everybody can nominate such a person, usually a secondary school teacher or a university lecturer. And many former students keep in touch with that person, partly out of thanks, and partly looking for continuing inspiration.

Often, the best teachers are not among the most successful from a career point of view. Nor are they necessarily the "Mr Chips" of the school. Inspirational teachers in universities probably spend too little time in library and laboratory scribbling for those all-important publications that are necessary for promotion. Some don't care for high (management) positions because they know where both their strengths and their joys lie. They generally like their students, preferring bright, energetic, forward-looking young people to their sour, political and jealous colleagues.

*The History Boys*, by Alan Bennett, is a play (later a movie) about inspirational teachers. It contrasted the eccentric and intrinsically motivated teacher with the pragmatic and extrinsic type. It was clear whom you were to admire and whom to despise. It was a critique of the modern obsession with grades, which encourages superficial, achievement-oriented as opposed to deep learning. The aim these days is to grade achievement, not understanding; the ability to satisfy examiners, not the imagination.

So what are the characteristics of the inspirational teacher? *First*, there is unbounded *enthusiasm*, even *passion*, for their subject. They demonstrate the thrill, the joy and the sheer pleasure of acquiring skills and knowledge in a particular area. And they are able to communicate this. Indeed, they can't hide it. It's not easy to fake passion – or at least not over a sustained period. All great teachers are passionate. Work becomes play with them. The motivation is purely intrinsic.

*Second*, they are *evangelists,* trying to convert minds rather than achieve exam-oriented goals. They want others to share their joy and passion, believing it is good for the students. They really want to communicate the good news. One of the characteristics of the inspirational teacher is that they never retire. They don't want to, and nor do their employers want them to. They are simply too valuable. And good administrators know this. They soon become "emeritus" but usually eschew the title, preferring simply to carry on ignoring the passing of the years.

*Third*, they *set high standards*. Inspirational teachers are not merely benevolent, kindly parental substitutes. They have the highest expectations of people. They do not compromise, but they do encourage. They teach the "hard stuff" but in a way that it can be grasped. They understand the learning process and the markers along the way. They are thus able to get the best out of people, and it is often for this that they are profoundly admired. They know what individual students are capable of, and strive to help them achieve their potential.

*Fourth*, they *update their material,* metaphors and messages. Every generation needs a different introduction to the discipline. They come with different experiences and expectations. Their hot (and cold) buttons are different. They need to be approached differently. The inspirational teacher is thus always in fashion, and able to appeal to many throughout their careers. It goes without saying that they have to update their knowledge as well.

Fifth, there is the issue of *adaptation* and *flexibility*. This means knowing how to "package the brand" differently to appeal to different individuals and generations. The intelligence, social backgrounds and values of students dictate that they have to be addressed differently. Brilliant teachers can, and do, this.

There is a current fashion for executive coaches in business. A great teacher is, of course, both a coach and a role model. All great teachers bring their topic alive by constant reference to current events and how knowledge of the subject will enable students to better understand the world around them. They show the subject's relevance.

Are work-based trainers in the same category? Sometimes. People in training companies do enter-trainment and edu-tainment well because they know the reaction on the happy sheets determines whether they are re-employed. But training at work is often too short-term, too skill focused and too pragmatic to have great teachers wanting to become great trainers.

Inspirational teachers inspire by intrinsic motivation. Their students will voluntarily stay on after school, write essays that "don't count," and do additional reading. Such teachers paint the big picture, and direct students to excellent sources.

Skills-based teaching, as in the performing arts, crafts and technology, is no different. Students apprenticed to a master will often acknowledge their amazing insight and dedication to shaping their skills. It is no accident that the "master-class" is so popular in business.

And why are inspirational teachers the way they are? Intelligent, knowledgeable, multi-skilled, all of these. But most say they became teachers or lecturers because they themselves had an inspirational teacher. So it's not genetic … but it certainly is passed on.

# Interview techniques

Why do books concerned to teach "killer interview questions" sell? To outfox and outgun the smarmy, over-confident interviewee? Perhaps. But there now exist just as many books that provide "brilliant answers" to tough questions. So both parties now come armed into the smoke-and-mirrors charade called the job interview. And, as in war, the first casualty is truth. Some interviewers see the event as a PR opportunity. Others as an impression wrestling match. And a few as a fact-finding mission.

Clever interviewees prepare. Some use CV professionals and studio photographs. They dress up. They do their homework and research relevant company details on the internet. They learn to "play back" the myths, deceptions and fairy tales the company projects. Just as good lawyers know never to ask a question of which they don't know the answer, so good interviewees like to come to the interview knowing what the questions will be ... and the smart answers.

One poll by Hirescore (in a press release of 2010) found that a surprisingly large number of people admitted lying in interviews: 67 percent about their salary in their previous job; 61 percent about qualifications; 58 percent about relevant experience; 54 percent about the reason for leaving the previous employment; 52 percent about commitment to their career; 36 percent about job titles in previous roles; and even 32 percent about marital status.

Interview techniques seem to fall under three headings: special techniques, selective memories, and responsibility issues. Some of the techniques amount to little more than vulgar *self-promotion*. Young people now have a paragraph before their simple, biographical details in which they say things like "I am a hard worker" or "I am energetic and motivated." Perhaps it is the interviewer's jobs to assess the extent to which this may be true. Interviewees learn to tell personal fables: stories of their heroic Stakhanovite contribution, their selflessness and sensitivity. Well rehearsed and told enthusiastically.

Apart from puffing themselves up, they often do what is called "*other enhancement*." Here they flatter, praise or compliment the interviewer or the organization: "I have certainly noticed your impressive rise in share price/market share/award getting." It's a bit tricky trying to compliment the interviewers as this smarmy, ingratiating sycophancy may really backfire.

Some attempt this non-verbally, almost in a flirty way; a dangerous technique, but it can be powerful in the right circumstances.

Next there is *opinion conformity*: "like me, like you." This is expressing beliefs that the interviewee assumes the interviewer has. Or agreeing with something the interviewer says. We like people who are like us: the similarity effect. This can happily be exploited.

The selective memory has a number of manifestations, but simply is just as much about selective forgetting. One is about *overcoming obstacles*: students who did well despite (a) having a part-time job; (b) looking after a sick mother; (c) working in a third language; or (d) doing it all by distance learning.

Equally, there is the *enhancement issue*: claiming that some positive event was in fact much more positive than in reality; for example, a claim such as "Not only did I turn around the department, but this started a whole range of initiatives, with other departments following my example."

Expert CV readers are always looking for gaps – missing years; or the omission of some obvious factors. Often it's easier to conceal than to lie, so selective forgetting is more common than selective enhancement.

The third area is responsibility issues. These come under the headings of excuses, justification and entitlement.

*Excuses* amount to little more than denying responsibility for one's actions. So "They never sent me the form;" "I was on sick leave during that period"; "I had a supervisor who was little more than a bully."

*Justifications* amount to accepting responsibility for poor performance but minimizing its effects: "We didn't win the contract but had a very good learning experience."

But the most common area is *entitlement*. This is over-claiming (personal) responsibility for past successes, ignoring the role of subordinates, lucky circumstance (the market), and any other individuals in the business. At worst this is narcissistic self-aggrandisement; and at best pathetic and delusional.

So the well-practiced interviewee comes equipped with a range of stories, rationales and techniques designed to impress. No wonder so many selection errors occur. But two questions follow from this. Impression management is a skill and particularly useful in some parts of the business (for example, sales and marketing). So the better they do this at interview, the better they might be at the job? And might, at times, these skills be an asset? But perhaps they could equally conceal some rather undesirable pathologies.

More important, how to prevent interviewee impression management interfering with making good selection decisions? The answer lies in a structured application form and a structured interview, but equally important, a structured interview for referees. Don't do the lazy thing of sending a job description to the referees nominated by the interviewee, which is itself often a clever ploy.

Do your homework. Find six people crucial in the candidate's past life and call them. Be sure what you want to know and why, and ask them the questions. Organizations that are nervous about references seem less stuffy about non-recorded telephone calls. And it's much easier for the referees who really know the truth.

The clearer you are about what you want in an interviewee and what those markers are, the easier it is to draw up a set of questions for both the interviewee and the referee.

# The leader profit chain

Various business concepts, including the *Service Profit Chain* and the *Gallup Path Model*, propose a direct link between the management styles of senior leaders and the company's actual profitability. It seems self-evident that companies with good management practices are, in the long-term, more profitable. And that it is senior managers who determine and ensure that good management practices are used.

The chain idea is that the long-term survival and profitability come from happy repeat customers who value the service and product they consistently receive. Particularly good service, is marked by attentive, knowledgeable, reliable and self-evidently happy staff. It is not that difficult to spot an alienated, discontented, jobsworth staffer, or the opposite: a cheery, go-the-extra-mile enthusiast. The end of the chain is sustainable profit, driven by happy repeat customers. They return because they get what they want, and more. And they are served by happy and productive staff, who are not there by chance but as a result of the way in which they have been selected, rewarded and supported: in short, managed. Their senior leaders have vision, strategy and skills. Hence the chain from leadership to profitability.

Various attempts have been made to monetize leadership. One study done in the early 1990s suggested that a high-performing senior executive of a big multinational, compared to an average or mediocre leader, could add as much as £10 million to the bottom line. Another, more recent, study estimated that around one-sixth (16 percent) to one-fifth (20 percent) of the variability in a company's performance is related to the behavior, personality and style of the CEO.

Perhaps it's easier to estimate the cost of bad management in terms of absenteeism, turnover and missed opportunities, not to mention poor PR, brand tarnishing and falling share price. That is, costs are a more reliable index of bad management than benefits. But it is impossible to monetize other, more subtle, effects, such as missed opportunities or the loss of knowledge workers.

Bad leaders are deceitful, greedy and manipulative. They often model all the values that lead to a doom-determined culture. "Political," devious and back-stabbing interactions become the norm. The good people become cynical and disheartened, and leave. There is truth in the saying, when applied to management, that fish rot from the head first.

It is the lethal but common combination of personality characteristics that produce the narcissistic, Machiavellian, psychopathic leader, and paradoxically, it is this combination that serves them so well. They have all the self-confidence to do well and impress others, which is increased if they are in any way articulate and good-looking. And it is the "integrity-lite" aspect of the psychopath that allows and encourages all the "ducking and weaving" that it takes to get to the top. The Machiavellianism is often thought of as strong, bold, no-nonsense leadership.

The task of a leader is to form, direct and support high-performing teams to execute a well-thought-out strategy. Leaders don't have to be liked, though they do have to be respected. Crucially they need to be people of the heart and the head: to have both technical and people skills.

Back in 2005, a *Harvard Business Review* article (Casciaro and Lobo 2005) appeared about "competent jerks and lovable fools." The idea is that you need IQ (competence) and EQ (likeability) to be any good. The competent jerk had high technical but low people skills, and the loveable fool the reverse. Of course, you need both ... but often at different stages of the climb to the top. Initially, technical skill and knowledge are essential to get the job, but the emotional intelligence requirement "clicks in" as soon as any supervisory or management responsibility is demanded.

An organizational culture is a set of practices that is directly and indirectly endorsed and modelled by senior management. It can hit you like a brick when you visit the organization headquarters, with its attitudes to security, to authority and to achievement. What the mission statement says may be just PR. It's what people do that counts. Most corporate cultures can be traced back to powerful early leaders who imposed their work preferences and values on the organization: the successful ones thrived.

Perhaps a good current case of the founder's influence on the organizational culture is seen in Morrison's Supermarket. Dalton Philips, the CEO at the time of writing, runs the fourth-largest supermarket chain in Britain, which, despite having absorbed the Safeway chain, remained without a fully integrated IT system for stock control because Sir Ken Morrison did not believe in full computerization. He also preferred to be on the shop floor and to stay in touch with his managers and staff. This attitude to computers was so ingrained in the culture that it persisted throughout the four-year tenure of the first non-family CEO, Marc Bolland.

The fragility of the chain is manifest most clearly at the start. The starter/founder/originator often casts a long shadow: a set of beliefs, values and practices that can easily outlive their usefulness if the founder begins to get a little overconfident or rigid. This is often a legacy that can be unwelcome.

## Reference

Casciaro, T. and Lobo, M.S. (2005) "Competent Jerks, Lovable Fools, and the Formation of Social Networks," *Harvard Business Review*, 83(6).

# The legacy problem

As the evening of one's life draws in, thoughts inevitably turn to what it has all meant, what is coming next, and how one will be remembered. Politicians, business tycoons and celebrities fret over their reputations. For some, the climb up the greasy pole has left a large number of envious enemies waiting to see them fall from grace.

There are three standard "solutions" to the problem of death and immortality. The *first* is *religion*. Many possible brand choices, with a variety of, albeit rather vague, promises of eternal life. Some say you return to this world, others hold the promise of paradise. It's a good solution if you buy the package, though it's all a bit of a risk.

The religion solution also seems to have some costs. It's not good enough, it seems, on one's deathbed to renounce the materialism, selfishness and hedonism that have characterized one's life up to that point. And this metaphysical solution speaks little to one's legacy. You might "live on," but what about protecting, enhancing or cherishing one's memory in those who remain and in future generations?

The *second* is *genetic*. By having children the survival of some genes is guaranteed. Further, children can be shaped from an early age to share their parents' values, vision and virtues. The next best thing is to form a tight family unit, hoping that the wider clan will protect one's legacy.

Many a business person will describe the folly of this approach. You roll the dice with children. All parents "believe" in genetics for their first child, but give up the idea when the second one appears and is so different. It's very rare that family businesses last more than three generations. Relatives fall out with each other: "God gave us our friends and the Devil our relations" is a well-known saying.

In fact, given the number of "confessional books" around and the number of repressed memory court cases, it may seem that children are a distinct handicap, not only in following the parental path but also in protecting one's memory.

So that leaves the *third* solution. This is *legacy management* before death, hoping to cheat the Grim Reaper's ability to induce amnesia in the living. Politicians agonize about how to do this, as do enormously successful business people who have time and money to spare after they have put all their affairs in order.

First, there is the book. We know history is written by victors. For some – for example, prime ministers and presidents – it is not only a course requirement but also a very serious source of income. It is so important to some politicians that they start writing, in effect, the day they are selected. They remember well the idea: you keep a diary and later it keeps you.

And if you don't release all the relevant papers at the time of the event you may have many hitherto unseen historical documents to support your case. Hence the self-serving, egotistical and one-sided nature of hagiographic autobiographies.

Business people, even if relatively famous, are not always so lucky with their published works. Unless they appear on television a great deal, fewer people will buy the thoughts and life of the CEO of Acme Widgets, however much money he or she made. John Harvey-Jones, Jack Welsh and the panel members in *The Dragons' Den* wrote books tied to their TV fame.

The book solution is too daunting for many who can't really write. The ghost-written solution sometimes works, but then the whole thing often seems bland. It's no wonder that charity shops are full of such dull, hardly read and never reprinted books of the great and the good from the past.

Next there is architecture. Build a monument to oneself. It worked for Christopher Wren and Gustave Eiffel. But even iconic buildings can be demolished. Try to find any London building put up in the 1970s that is worth preserving. The building approach is also very expensive and often guarantees little more than the memory of a name, let alone what the person believed in or stood for.

What about the *scholarship fund*? Such as Rhodes scholarships, Nobel Prize winners; or a *charity* such as the Leonard Cheshire Disability care homes or Macmillan Cancer Support? This is perhaps the preferred solution of the super-rich. Bill Gates, Oprah Winfrey and Warren Buffet have chosen this method. What do they have in common? A lot of money.

But even this method is not immune to fashion. Some universities have great problems with scholarships to be awarded to the "top woman student", or worse, "top boy from Southern Sudan". Witness the current problem of atheists accepting the (almost unknown) Templeton Prize, now worth a lot more than the Nobel Prize.

How about the *endowed chair* in a university? Or better, a whole business school named after you. This is very popular in America, where even the most obscure business school from Nowhereville, Fly-Over State

University is endowed by the local entrepreneurs who did well. An expensive option. And what if all you can afford is an institution in the bottom division?

Perhaps there is a paradox, or even a parable, in this whole issue. The harder you try to ensure your legacy, the less successful you will be. People will smell a rat, and suspect manipulation. Perhaps the truth is what you should have learned in Sunday School: it is only a long, virtuous and selfless life that guarantees its just reputational reward. Alas, that is not true either. Think of all those who still worship Joseph Stalin. Or what we now know about John F. Kennedy and choose to forget.

Perhaps all the talk about change at work means that nothing lasts very long in the world of business or economics. Best then to live in the present and not attempt to shape the future.

# Lie detectors

Lie detection is serious business. While there are a lot of "body language experts" – self-appointed gurus who claim to have considerable skill and accuracy in detecting lies, the data say otherwise. Gaze avoidance, nose touching and squirming in a chair are indeed associated with lying – but also with general anxiety about being interviewed.

It is common to hear various claims about the power and importance of non-verbal language. To back it up, some even express it in percentages. So one is told that 93 percent of the information communicated in face-to-face meetings is non-verbal. Most of it is through face and body movements and expressions, and around a third is derived from voice quality and tone.

The lowest percentage is always assigned to verbal communication, the words that people actually say. This is, of course, patent nonsense: why would anyone bother to learn a foreign language when they could be communicating with 90 percent efficiency non-verbally? Sure, we "leak" non-verbal cues when we lie: but it is better to listen to what is being said.

Usually, lying is hard work. Not the kind of "white-lie" lying intended to avoid social embarrassment and injured feelings, but serious lying with serious consequences. Claiming to have done things you didn't do, or to have been somewhere else when you were actually present at a significant event.

Lying is difficult and demanding, because the liar has to do several things at the same time:

1. To get the story right: it must be plausible and consistent with all known (revealed and revealable) facts.
2. To memorize the story well so that the liar is completely consistent in retelling it many times while possibly being recorded.
3. To scrutinize the interlocutors to ensure they are swallowing the bait.
4. To memorize the script and to perform: the emotions displayed need to match the story. This takes effort.
5. In addition to remembering the script the liar also has to repress or suppress memories of the actual occurrence.

So it takes a good memory, acting skills, emotional intelligence and sheer effort to tell a lie (many times) convincingly and get away with it. That is why experts talk of "duping delight" – catching liars after the event when they are suddenly relieved and relaxed after their performance has ended.

Some experts in the field of lie detection who published a study (Vrij *et al.* 2011) in *Current Directions in Psychological Science*, which utilized the idea of increased "cognitive load." They recommend some pretty nifty tricks to catch out liars. Many of these are, of course, well known to the experts, who also know how difficult it is to catch out liars simply by observing them because the cues are faint, subtle and unreliable.

1. **Tell the story in reverse order**
   It's not that easy to do, but much easier if the story has not been fabricated. Sequences are not always well thought through by liars and the fumbling and bumbling can soon be spotted.
2. **Maintain eye contact in the telling**
   Liars have to concentrate inwards. Other people are arresting and distracting. The gaze of liars often shifts to motionless objects as they "go inwards." Maintaining eye contact is very difficult if you are trying to remember your lines.
3. **Using unanticipated questions**
   Liars are sensitive to saying "I do not recall/remember/know." It sounds fishy. So they learn to give plausible answers. So ask questions they don't expect and ask them more than once. If they lie about a meal, ask them what the other person ordered, who finished first, where their table was. Ask them about colors, smells, incidentals. Ask the same question again, phrased differently. Get them to draw a room and look for details.
4. **Devil's advocate**
   A lot of lies are about opinions and beliefs. Good liars are usually able to articulate a clear ideological position. So ask them to be the Devil's advocate, in effect providing their true opinions about an issue. Liars are faster at this and give richer, more complex answers than those who are telling the truth.
5. **Strategic questioning**
   Most liars have to do avoidance and denial. They need a number of strategies to avoid having to admit or describe true events, as well as denial strategies. Innocent people say more, fearing interviewers do not have all the facts; guilty people say less for fear of incrimination. So clever interviewers ask open followed by closed questions. Innocent people are more likely to offer facts spontaneously than are liars.

The use of these and other specific techniques depends on the situation, the crime and the preferences of the lie detectors. The trouble with lying is that to be successful one has to be skillful, determined and well prepared. It helps to have a weak conscience: those who do, do not leak signs of their lying as much as those with a well-developed super-ego.

The trick for the lie detector is to make it difficult for the liar to continue with the lie. He or she has to be smart to outsmart the professional detectors. And learning how the professionals work might help the liar to do it better.

## Reference

Vrij, A., Granhag, P., Mann, P. and Leal, S. (2011) "Outsmarting the Liars," *Current Directions in Psychological Science*, 20: 28–32.

# Loafers, suckers and free-riders

There are many really wonderful benefits of meetings. One is an opportunity to have "time-out" while looking conscientious. Meetings take minutes but waste hours. You can write shopping lists, looking as if you are scrupulously taking notes. You can gaze earnestly at slides while thinking about holiday plans. You can surreptitiously do some Blackberrying without many noticing.

It is surprising how great a percentage of a (senior) manager's day is "caught up" in meetings of all sorts. Many move from one to another getting ever so slightly more dazed and bewildered as they potter along. There are all sorts of reasons for having meetings. They supposedly improve decision-making, but more important, of course, they are about diffusion of responsibility if the decision is a poor one.

Decisions made in groups are, paradoxically, often more extreme than those made by individuals. We used to think that groups moderated decisions: made them likely to adopt the middle way, more "tolerant," more cautious. In fact, the data suggest the opposite. Groups apparently shift people to extremes of risk and caution.

Some managers wisely refuse to attend any meeting that does not have an agenda. An agenda is a map, a menu: a sign that the meeting has at least been planned. And if you don't like what is on the menu, you don't attend. The agenda is also a running order so attendees can judge when to arrive and when to leave. This may be very naïve, of course, because we all know about hidden agendas!

There has been good evidence for 100 years that people often put less effort into a task when they work in a team or group than they would when working alone. It's called social loafing. It was demonstrated by a German researcher, who measured big, strong chaps pulling ropes. First, he established their typical strength of pull. Then he put them in a tug-of-war, and measured it again. The force exerted by the team was nearly always less than the aggregated pull of the individuals. Many arms make weak pull: somehow they experienced co-ordination or motivation loss.

Social loafing does take place. The question is why and when, and perhaps more important, what we can do about it to prevent that all-important productivity loss.

The *first* explanation is that in some way the pressure is off, or at least lessened. The pressure to complete a task that people feel as group members seems less intense than when working on the task alone. *Second*, and related to this, the presence of group members is "drive-reducing" because the responsibility for carrying out the task is inevitably shared. *Third*, there is always reduced identifiability in collective versus individual actions: it is harder to describe how much effort was put in by individuals. *Fourth*, it can also happen that people in groups feel less essential and more dispensable in terms of the effectiveness of their contribution.

Groups can encourage a diffusion of responsibility. That is why people in need are less likely to be helped in crowded spaces and big towns than in relatively empty places. Let others do the helping. And so you notice what appears to be a callous disregard for the welfare of others.

Social loafing is seen nicely in brainstorming groups, where those disinclined to take part in the fun-and-frolics volunteer to scribble on the flip chart, so counting themselves out of the real activity of generating creative ideas.

Some people love the exhilaration of being a free-rider. That is, joining hard-working and effective groups to enjoy the benefits of their success but without pulling their weight. Free-riders are serial social loafers. And this can lead to the formation of two groups: real and pseudo workers – those who pull their weight and those who are pulled. The danger is that the real workers discover they are suckers. They have been victims of free-loaders, and themselves soon become demotivated and demoralized.

Is social loafing an individual or a corporate culture issue? That is, does it vary according to an individual's personality and values? Disagreeable, selfish cynics versus empathic, conscientious and trusting individuals?

Or is it more likely to be a function of the corporate culture: the norms established in organizations with complacent overmanning, the invention of non-jobs and the general acceptance of social loafing? The answer is probably both.

So how best to deal with social loafing, given that it is often quite a serious problem? Ideally this involves being able to identify and evaluate (meaning measure) an individual's contribution to group tasks. It is best if you can ensure the uniqueness of an individual's input. It can help to have ways of providing feedback on both individual and group performance.

Social loafing is less likely to occur in smaller rather than bigger groups, so it may be advisable to break up large groups. It also occurs less where the tasks are more meaningful for individuals and more self-involving. That means enriching the tasks – which, admittedly, is not always possible.

And social loafing occurs less when people in groups have close ties: bonds of affection and friendship. Groups with no social cohesion descend to become suckers and loafers who never really like, trust or feel responsible for each other.

# Market research

It has been said the Blair and Brown Labour Governments in Britain spent vast sums of taxpayers' money on focus groups trying to find out what the person-in-the-voting-booth really thought. The idea was to pick up on popular issues, concerns, values and the like and "spin" them away with clever marketing. The world knows the result.

The central idea of the focus group is to hear the language and ideas of ordinary people. The product of focus groups is usually a report, differing enormously in length, style and depth. These reports are characterized by having many quotes from participants and by the essentially wry, perceptive interpretations of the observer on what, how and why ideas were generated.

There are various important critiques of focus groups. Generalizations cannot be made from these small, deliberately unrepresentative, samples. Results are desperately unreliable. Run two groups and you will get quite different results. Have different moderators and interpreters for the same group and you will also have two very different reports. In short, the results are not replicable.

Public ideas are problematic, pluralistic, conflicting, diverse and contradictory. The focus group stresses (indeed, often rejoices) in this and yields results that are of no help to the decision-maker. Rather than clarifying the situation, they tend to make it worse. In a sense, the reports rejoice in indecisiveness and plurality, rather than consensus.

Even the most skilled moderator cannot overcome the fundamental problem of groups making decisions, because:

- People have evaluation apprehension – some self-censor, being scared about looking foolish, so will never say in a public forum (the very open focus group) what they really think.
- Social loafers will go along for the spectacle and the freebies but contribute little, letting the garrulous individuals speak for them. In this sense, the focus group reports are biased toward the eloquent and opinionated, who might or might not speak for the group.
- It is difficult to think about a problem seriously when some know-all is talking continually.

- There are powerful conformity pressures to take sides and follow certain individuals or subgroups; in short, to obey explicitly and implicitly upheld norms, giving a misleading idea of the spread of ideas in the group.

But there are, of course, other forms of market research. One is to question people standing on street corners or invite them to places to show them products or to watch videos. However, both behavioral economists and psychologists have demonstrated numerous artifacts that can really shape the outcome. These can, of course, be used by clever researchers to get the answer they want.

Consider just two issues. The first is called framing and it has powerful effects. Do you want to influence people's attitude to global warming? One researcher asked three groups to watch a movie on global warming in three different rooms: one was hot, another "normal," and a third cool. As predicted, those in the hot room thought it was a more serious issue than those who watched it in either of the other rooms.

In another celebrated study, people were asked to interview a candidate or watch an interview. Some were given a hot drink, others a cold drink just before rating the competence and suitability of the candidate. And the result? Those who held and drank from the hot cup found the candidate "warmer" and more suitable than those who were exposed to the cold drink.

The most common use of this technique is to give people the same information but expressed either as a loss or a gain. The same information; same data; same consequences, but if expressed as a loss, people will act. If you want people to pay a fee, warn them about the penalty fee for being late rather than the advantage discount of paying very early.

And there is another charming and very simple effect that can have great consequences. This refers simply to the phrasing order in which questions are asked. We know many things about how questioning affects the answers given. We know that specific questions are better than general questions. We know that closed questions are usually preferable to open ones. We know it helps to offer a "no opinion" or "I don't know" option. We know never to have an uneven scale because no one knows what the midpoint means (both, neither, not sure, average). It's better to offer forced choice (either/or) than agree/disagree.

But questionnaire order, irrespective of wording, can really make a difference to results. Consider "Rate your general life satisfaction" and

"Rate your marital life satisfaction." If these are rated in that order the correlation is $r = 0.3$, but in the reverse order $r = 0.6$.

In one famous study published 30 years ago, people were asked about abortion and whether a particular pregnant woman should be able to obtain legal, safe abortion. In (a) she is married and does not want any more children; and (b) there is a strong chance of a genetic defect in the baby. If you ask (b) before (a), many fewer people endorse (a).

The moral of the story? Many artifacts or biases occur in research. Well-informed but possibly dubious people can manipulate certain aspects to get the answer they want.

# Mentoring at work

Leaders have to bring out the best in their people. They need to know how to help others achieve their full potential. There are certainly many ways of helping people at work to flourish, grow and achieve their ambitions.

Consider the following C words:

*Coach*: Private tutor. One who instructs or trains a performer or sports player. To train intensively by instructions, demonstration and practice.

*Confessor*: A person who gives evidence of religious faith. A priest who hears confession is one's regular spiritual guide.

*Confidant(e)*: One to whom secrets are entrusted.

*Consultant*: An expert who gives professional advice or provides services.

*Counselor*: A person who gives professional, personal and perspicacious advice.

Then there are the T words:

*Teacher*: One who teaches or instructs.

*Therapist*: A person trained in methods of treatment and rehabilitative methods other than by the use of drugs or surgery.

*Trainer*: Someone who trains a person being prepared for a test or contest and bringing a desired degree of proficiency in a specified activity or skill.

There are also M words:

*Mentor*: One who provides disinterested, wise support.

*Moral tutor*: an upstanding, disinteresting referee.

*Master class*: A series of seminars in the tradition of old masters of apprentices.

*MBA*: An extremely expensive and time-consuming quest for a certificate that ensures a handsome payback.

One of the most cost-effective and beneficial things any good interpersonal manager, leader or supervisor can do is to offer mentoring. The word comes from Homer's Odyssey, where Mentor was a tutor to Odysseus's son, Telemachus. Mentor was a "wise and trusted advisor." The concept of mentoring is pretty straightforward, though there are various different definitions and lists of things that mentor and mentee/protégé should/shouldn't/need to do.

The idea is that (young) people new to an organization need help, advice and nurturing. Mentoring is about education, support and encouragement. And it's cheap! The plan is quite simply that mentor and protégé meet regularly to discuss business issues so that the latter learns to perform at the maximum of their potential as quickly as possible. Some organizations facilitate and support (even demand) mentoring. They make employee development a priority and offer formal rewards to those who engage in mentoring.

The mentoring process, then, is where an experienced, more senior supervisor/leader is committed to providing developmental assistance, guidance and support to a less experienced protégé. Mentors can (and should) provide their protégés with coaching, challenging assignments, exposure, protection and sponsorship. More than a cosy gossip now and again.

Different people have produced different recommendations about the "rules of engagement" when it comes to mentoring. Thus they should first establish the goals, and rules to play by; they need to model all desirable behaviors; they need to be as impartial and nonjudgmental as possible. Their task is to build awareness and confidence, extend analytical skills and deepen, strengthen and expand networks both within and outside the organization.

But it is *not* their job to become a personal therapist and try to sort out the mentee's psychological problems and personal relationships. It is not their primary task to get the mentee promoted. They are not there to be directive, prescriptive or proscriptive. Or, for that matter, to give business advice.

There are benefits to the mentor as well as the mentee. They have "stepchildren" in the organization. They stay in touch with another generation and they learn from them. They grow their influence base from below.

There are costs and benefits to mentoring. Mentees develop feelings of accomplishment and a sense of competence in addition to gaining new perspectives and knowledge. Mentors too acquire new (often technological) skills, support and an ally in their mentee. Mentors often talk of feelings of quasi-immortality watching their protégés grow and succeed.

There are costs if the relationship turns sour, though. Mentors have talked of exploitation and back-stabbing. Others perceive the time and effort expended as not worth it. Some mentors have also been accused of nepotism by jealous, non-mentored people.

However, there is evidence to suggest that if the programme is voluntary on both sides, the two are well matched, the mentor is trained and there is management support for the whole process, then mentoring can be a great success.

A central question is how an organization chooses and trains potential mentors among senior staff, and how they get matched up to their mentees. Not everyone is cut out to be a good mentor. Nearly all need some training in basic skills.

One question is how mentor and mentee are paired. What is the criterion? Who makes the decision: a learning and development specialist, the mentor, the mentee, the mentee's boss? Should there be some sort of speed-dating exercise to allow mentor and mentee to have a good "sniff around" one another. How does one ensure that the process is standardized across the organization? Should it be voluntary or compulsory?

So is mentoring a cost-effective development process that allows organizations to monitor and control the training they give to their young people? Is it preferable to the idea of external coaches of all shapes and sizes swarming in, over and around organizations with their massive invoices? Often; but it is important to get the process right. And there is always the problem of who mentors the senior mentors.

# Money as a motivator

Where do you stand on the issue of money as a motivator at work?

1. *For*: Money is an effective, powerful and simple motivator. Self-evidently, money motivates and extra money motivates people to work extra hard. It's natural to compete, and when rewarded with money for better work then productivity and standards are raised for all. Further, because it is not always wise or indeed possible to promote individuals, money can be used as an equitable and very acceptable way to reward all workers. More important, because money is a "generalized reinforcer" it is *always* acceptable to *all* people *everywhere* and at *all* times. Money talks, and it talks loudly and clearly.

2. *Equivocal*: Money sometimes, but not always, motivates. For those who are very well paid, even quite large amounts have a minimal motivational effect. Worse, money rewards can and do set employees against one another, leading to conflict, disharmony and reduced teamwork. It leads as much to a win–lose as a win–win philosophy. Also, it is very difficult in many jobs to determine or measure an individual's work performance accurately and equitably to decide how much money to award.

3. *Against*: Money is not effective and only has the power to demotivate. Money actually trivializes work: it turns those who are intrinsically motivated at work into extrinsically motivated workers. Money rewards (bonuses, performance-related pay) may bear little relation to what the worker does, or feels. If money works and is so motivating, perhaps the base salaries are too low. There are better ways to motivate people, other than cold cash. It is a naive nonsense to believe that if a person's salary is increased by, say, 20 percent this will generate a 20 percent increase in his/her productivity (or even morale).

There are at least four reasons why money is seen by business psychologists as being much more likely to be a cause of dissatisfaction than satisfaction. They argue that money does indeed have motivational effects, but that they are nearly all exclusively negative.

The *first* reason relates to the idea that the effects of a pay rise soon wear off as people adapt to their new conditions. Any improvements are therefore likely to be temporary. It can take as little as two to three months for people to "settle down" to their new situation. Money can be a very effective motivator but a great deal of it is needed to stop adaptation effects; too much for most organizations to bear.

*Second*, what leads to pay satisfaction is not so much absolute salary but rather comparative salary. So if my salary goes up dramatically, but so does that of my comparison group, there is no change in my behavior. The question, of course, is who my comparison group are, and do I really know what they actually receive. This is crucial and relates to the whole problem of performance-related pay, as we shall see. No matter what people are paid, if they believe, with or without evidence, that they are not being paid *equitably and fairly*, they become demotivated. And the smallest differential can have a great effect. That is why reading the appointment pages can generate such a lot of passion.

*Third*, money is not everything; in fact, it maybe much less important than health or holidays, time with the family or job security. Here is a choice: would you take £1,000 (immediate payment) or a week's extra holiday? Many would be happy with more time off or more job security than more money. People are prepared to *trade off* other things for money once they have enough, or grow weary of the game that is not worth the candle. The young, the desperate, perhaps the greedy, are willing to do anything for money. But are they the people on your payroll, or the people whom you want to employ?

*Finally*, there is the eternal implication of tax and spend ... all very well to increase pay, but if increased taxes eat heavily into it there can only be a marginal benefit. Why earn when the government take too much away from you? If the government takes 50 per cent or more ... working is hardly worth the effort.

The greatest shock is provided by the data from what is called the Easterlin hypothesis (see Easterlin 1980). This was a study that examined aggregated data collected over 50 years in America. While GDP had been growing steadily over the years, response levels regarding personal happiness had remained pretty stable. This led economists (yes, the dismal scientists) to attempt to calculate how much money is needed to *maximize a person's wellbeing*. The question is, what is the sum, expressed as an annual salary, beyond which an individual gets no "bang for his/her buck" in terms of happiness, well-being and contentment? What do you think: £100K, twice or thrice that? The answer is half that, or twice the average UK annual salary: around £50K.

Some reject this "factoid" as unbelievable nonsense; particularly those who chase elusive wealth all day long. They mistake the pursuit of money for the pursuit of happiness. They are certainly motivated to accumulate money quickly and feverishly so that they can quit their job and do something they really love.

### Reference

Easterlin, R. (1980) *Birth and Fortune*. New York: Basic Books.

# The narcissistic manager

Several versions of the myth of Narcissus survive. They are warnings about hubris and pride. Narcissus was the son of Cephissus, the river God. By the time he was 16 everyone recognized his ravishing beauty, but he scorned all lovers – of both sexes – because of his pride. The Goddess Nemesis arranged that Narcissus would stop to drink at a spring on the heights of Mount Helicon. As he looked in the water he saw his own reflection and instantly fell in love with the image. He could not embrace his reflection in the pool, but unable to tear himself away, he remained until he died of starvation. But no body remained – in his place was a flower.

Poets, painters and moralists have been intrigued with the myth and sought to interpret its meaning. The Freudians found the myth beguiling and looked for intrapsychic and psychopathological interpretations. There have also been various illuminating psychological accounts of famous plays such as Arthur Miller's (1949) *Death of a Salesman* being a proto-typical tale of narcissism.

At the heart of the myth is the caution of misperception and self-love: the idea that inaccurate self-perceptions can lead to tragic and self-defeating consequences. There appears to be a moral, social and clinical debate about narcissism. The moral issue concerns the evil of hubris; the social issue the benefit or otherwise of modesty; and the clinical debate is about the consequence of misperception.

Psychologists have also attempted to measure narcissism and to distinguish it from a form of "high self esteem". It has various clear components. *First*, exploitativeness and entitlement: the complete belief that one is very good at and entitled to manipulate people for one's own ends. *Second*, the belief that one is extremely talented at leadership and all authority roles. *Third*, all that superiority and arrogance arising from the belief of being a "born leader" and quite simply better than others. *Fourth*, adolescent self-absorption and self-admiration: the belief that one is special and worthy of adoration and respect.

Pathologically over-self-confident managers really believe in themselves and their abilities. They have no doubt that they are unique and special, and that there is a reason for their being on this planet. They expect others to treat them well at all times.

They are fierce competitors, love getting to the top and enjoy staying there. They have no trouble visualizing themselves as the hero, the star, the best in their role, or the most accomplished in their field. They have a keen awareness of their own thoughts and feelings, and their overall inner state of being. They are certainly good at accepting compliments, praise and admiration gracefully and with self-possession. But they often have an emotional vulnerability regarding the negative feelings and assessments of others, which are deeply felt, though they may be handled with the narcissist's customary grace.

It should not be assumed that narcissism is necessarily a handicap in business. Indeed, the opposite may be true. If managers are articulate, educated and intelligent as well as good-looking, their narcissism maybe seen to be acceptable.

On the bright side, narcissists can be good delegators, good team builders and good deliverers. They can be good mentors and genuinely help others. However, subordinates soon learn that things go wrong if they do not follow certain rules;

- Everyone must acknowledge who is the boss and accept rank and hierarchical structure.
- They must be absolutely loyal and never complain, criticize or compete.They should never take the credit and always acknowledge that any success is primarily a result of the narcissist's talent, direction or insight.
- They should not expect the narcissist to be very interested in their personality, concerns or ambitions, but they must be very interested in the narcissist's issues.
- They have to be attentive, giving and always flattering. They need to be sensitive to the whims, needs and desires of the narcissistic manager without expecting reciprocity.
- Narcissistic managers can be mean, angry or petulant when crossed or slighted, and quickly express anger, so subordinates have to be careful when working with them.
- They need to be alert so that a narcissistic manager's self-preoccupation, need for approbation and grandiosity do not impede business judgment and decision-making.

The dark side of narcissistic managers is that they tend to have shallow, functional and uncommitted relationships. Because they are both needy and egocentric they tend not to make close, supportive friendship networks in the workplace. They can often feel empty and neglected as a result.

Narcissistic leaders may have short-term advantages but long-term disadvantages because their consistent and persistent efforts are aimed at enhancing their self-image, which leads to group clashes.

The question about narcissism is to what extent it helps with climbing the greasy pole in business but then later causes them to slip down the very pole they tried so hard to ascend. Everyone wants and admires self-confident managers with high self-esteem – comfortable in their own skin and aware of their own strengths. But success can lead to admiration and a distortion in feedback. Successful managers, blessed by hard-working staff and a successful organization in a growth market, may erroneously come to believe that they alone are the architects of their success. And this starts the process of delusions of grandeur that brings them down in the end.

# Nutters at work

The laws of supply and demand presumably apply as much to self-help books as to any other. And we all know from bitter personal experience of a boss, colleague or employee, that some people at work are seriously difficult. Difficult to manage, difficult to motivate and difficult to team up with. They suck up your time and attention and give little in return.

No wonder that people look for help in that most American of solutions: the magic self-help book. A quick survey of the Amazon website throws up the following snappy titles:

1. *Jerks at Work: How to Deal With People Problems and Problem People.*
2. *I Hate People: Kick loose from the overbearing and underhand jerks at work and get what you want out of your job.*
3. *Toxic Workplace: Managing Toxic Personalities and Their Systems of Power.*
4. *The No Asshole Rule: Building A Civilised Workplace and Surviving One That Isn't.*
5. *Dealing with People You Can't Stand: How to Bring Out the Best in People at their Worst.*
6. *Coping with Difficult People: The Proven-Effective Battle Plan That Has Helped Millions Deal with the Troublemakers in Their Lives at Home and at Work.*
7. *Since Strangling Isn't an Option... Dealing with Difficult People – Common Problems and Uncommon Solutions.*
8. *Toxic Co-workers: How to Deal with Dysfunctional People on the Job.*
9. *Coping with Toxic Managers, Subordinates ... and Other Difficult People by Using Emotional Intelligence to Survive and Prosper.*

Note that the books refer to *difficult* and *toxic* people. But, being American, where litigious parents sue their children (and vice versa) on *Judge Judy*, few would dare to imply that these difficult people might be more than difficult: more likely *dysfunctional* and *disturbed.* OK, out with it: suffering from a mental illness.

Given the incidence of mental illness in society, it would be highly surprising if we did not meet it every day. But how many people recognize someone with such an illness? Work on what is called *mental health literacy* indicates that most of us could recognize a person suffering from clinical depression, but far fewer could identify schizophrenia or bipolar disorder.

To be able to recognize a borderline or schizotypal personality disorder could be very useful. Indeed, there are (much better) popular books written by psychologists and psychiatrists that try to explain the behavior of those who have problems, mainly personality disorders, in our midst.

The first thing to do is to make the condition or diagnosis less mysterious by cutting out the jargonized psychobabble. So obsessive compulsives may be called overconscientious detailers, diligent or perfectionist. Equally, clinical narcissists could be called arrogant, bold pruners or super-self-confident.

Second, the books detail the typical behaviors associated with a particular condition. The aim is to help diagnosis. The behaviors are spelled out in detail. But the books are much "lighter" on how to cure the condition. In fact, they don't talk about cure, they talk about *management*. What to do if your boss/colleague/report (even spouse) is a passive aggressive, paranoid, histrionic personality? Clinicians seem a lot more pessimistic than managers or self-help book authors, who offer proven ways to solve the problem.

The most common and undiagnosed disorders associated with senior management are antisocial personality disorder (that is, being a psychopath) and narcissistic personality disorder. The guilt-free, manipulative, risk-taking but deceitful and cunning psychopath can flourish in many business settings, so much so that they are not thought of as being disturbed or dysfunctional at all. They are in some sectors the norm: so they are normal and the rest of the world is not!

But is all this talk a worrying trend among psychiatrists to medicalize and pathologize every form of behavior? So a naughty child in need of a spank has *oppositional defiant disorder* and needs psychotherapy on the NHS? Certainly there has been an asymptotic rise in the number of disorders "discovered" or demarcated by psychologists.

Yet *mental health literacy* brings many advantages. It is all about recognizing behaviors at work, or out of, for what they are. Most of all it helps to explain the origin of the problem as well as the best pathways to help. It gives a much better idea about prognosis and what sorts of treatments are likely to make the problem worse rather than better.

Try your skill: What is wrong with Laura?

Laura is a married 45-year-old lawyer. She is known as the hardest-driving member of the firm. She is too proud to turn down a new case and too much of a perfectionist to be satisfied with the work done by her assistants. Displeased by their writing style and sentence structure, she finds herself constantly correcting their briefs and is therefore unable to keep up with her schedule. When assignments become backed up, she cannot decide which to address first, starts making schedules for herself and her staff, but then is unable to meet them and starts working 15 hours a day. Laura never seems to be able to relax. Even on vacations, she develops elaborate activity schedules for every family member and gets angry and impatient if they refuse to follow her plans.

Answers on a postcard.

# The obsolescent CEO

Here's a hypothetical question: you are asked to vote for a new CEO. There are two final candidates, and they are surprisingly similar. They have near-identical educational qualifications, personality traits and values. They seem equally bright. But one is 35 and the other is 63 years old. Which would you choose? The dynamism and energy of youth, or the understanding and wisdom of maturity?

Most CEOs are between these hypothetical ages, usually five to eight years on either side of 50. So what is the essential difference? The answer is that very woolly concept known as *experience.* Age represents "seen it all before"; "tried and tested"; "all in good time"; while youth is "do keep upx"; "move with the times"; and "change or die."

So when is experience useful and relevant, and when is it not? What happens if the world has changed? There is nothing worse, and somehow rather pathetic, seeing the aging leader clinging on to the strategy, processes and procedures of a previous era that clearly do not work any more.

Experience can be a serious handicap. People have to *unlearn* lessons and obsolete technology, which may be harder than learning them in the first place. This is less true of people issues than processes. And how easy is it to train or teach older people new things?

Certainly governments who run pension schemes want to keep us at work, particularly in old (in both senses of the word) Europe. There are more older workers than ever before: nearly three times as many 40-, 50- and 60-year-olds in work than there were a hundred years ago. And there are quite simply not enough young people at work to pay for their generous pensions.

Around half of all Germans, two-thirds of Americans and three-quarters of Swiss people between the ages of 55 and 65 work full-time. In 1980, there were about twice as many under-30s as over-50s in the European workforce. It is predicted that this figure will reverse by the year 2020.

Do employers want older workers? Or young workers want older bosses? Are the latter slow, doddery, forgetful and computer phobic? Or are they more reliable, conscientious and good with customers? Are greying temples reassuring or something to worry about?

Studies do show that, quite naturally, older workers hold pretty positive views about their older peers. Interestingly, the quality and quantity of contact with older workers has very positive effects on younger workers' attitudes towards them. But older supervisors have more negative opinions about older workers than do younger supervisors.

So what are the issues? Potential loss of productivity is a concern. The evidence, however, is that if people are in reasonable health and in the right job for their temperament and values, there is no decline whatever in productivity up to the age of 80. What about older people's *lack of enthusiasm for change and innovation*? The able employee, given good continuing training, is not necessarily change-averse even at advanced ages. As much depends on the person's personality as on their declining abilities. Some 20-year-olds are massively change-averse; while some 80-year-olds are very willing to "have a go at something new."

By and large, older CEOs are bright, energetic and engaged: more so than many other people of their age. They are sometimes called *elite survivors*. They age well intellectually. It is not the knife or the hair dye: it is intellectual fitness and flexibility.

But what about their declining abilities? It is true that it may be harder to teach an old dog new tricks. Word fluency, memory, reasoning and speed of reactions do decline, but for most people this is only seriously noticeably after the age of 75.

Four things influence older workers' and managers' ability and productivity. First, their *physical and mental health,* which influence all aspects of their social functioning. Next, their *education and ability*. Third, their *motivation and attitude to work*. And finally, there is the *nature of the work* itself, with its peculiar and particular set of mental and physical demands.

Older people *can* bring wise judgment and social competence to an organization. Many have greater acceptance and credibility with customers, shareholders or journalists than do young people, and they have often built up useful and supportive networks both inside and outside the organization. Many enjoy and have become used to lifelong learning and continuing education: "Learning a little each day, makes it far easier to stay." And many still embrace the old-fashioned values of commitment and loyalty.

Teaching older people means applying what we know about adult education more carefully. Their education, under certain conditions, works best when they are taught with meaningful and familiar materials; can pace their own learning; have training on a weekly basis rather than in blocks; practice with new materials; and can call on special tutors and peers for help if necessary.

So what exactly is an "older" worker or manager? And at what age can we expect someone to peak in terms of management? We know what is true for athletes, but what about in the boardroom?

And so to the question posed at the start of this essay. CEOs need to be bright, hard-working and emotionally stable. They need integrity and courage, and the ability to learn. Perhaps it depends on the sector, though the late Steve Jobs of Apple was not young, he was innovative to the last, and continued to work despite battling for years with serious illness. Perhaps what fades in older people is the sheer hunger for success, the drive and ambition. As Meg Whitman (the former CEO of eBay) said, when searching for her successor: "Everyone I know is too rich and too tired."

# Peanuts and monkeys

If supervisors complain about the poor motivation of their staff and offer the "explanation" that *if you pay people peanuts, you get monkeys,* dismiss them immediately.

Well, first do two small checks: see if the de/unmotivated staff are paid competitively according to market rates; second, see if there is some concept of performance management in the organization, so that people have some agreed goals and targets, and a mechanism to provide feedback on how they are doing. If they are paid reasonably compared to the market and there are some standards of management (goal-setting, feedback and so on), then sack the peanut-monkey manager.

Peanut-monkey people are quite simply unskilled, unperceptive and/ or inadequately skilled for the job. It is most likely that they have been promoted from a technical job at which they did very well into a supervisory/management position which they don't like and doesn't suit their temperament. That means they are probably very low in charm, persuasion and influencing skills, and they lack socio-emotional skills. They have low "psychological-mindedness."

Peanut-money people find it difficult to respond well to a few simple questions. Ask them:

1. Whether the reverse proposition is true: *If you pay people in gold bars do you get Stakhanovites*? And, if not, why not?
2. How do you manage and motivate volunteers who receive nothing for their hard work?
3. Why two people in essentially the same job seem so different in terms of their motivation, morale and productivity?

The issue is understanding motivation: what makes any activity in and of itself fun, even addictive? How do you generate excitement and interest in people? It is probably predictable that peanut-monkey managers are the types who bribe (they call it incentivize) their children to do well in exams by offering cash payments. So, depending on the age of the child and the wealth (and stupidity) of (British) parents it may be, say, £100 for an A grade, £60 for a B and £30 for a C. Or perhaps an exciting £250 for an A*?

It is this logic that some parents apply to pocket-money rules. You get the money only if your room is tidy or all the toys are taken out of the living area. Pocket money is a wage for a set of behaviors. The rules apply to how you earn it, not how you spend it.

The problem with payment for results is that it turns education into a job, and tidiness into something you expect to be rewarded for. What happens to the child who goes on to university? Will he or she want a new reward system: and something much higher and grander to reflect what they have to do ... so £1,000 for a first and so on? Will it be possible ever to experience the love of learning for its own sake? It turns young people into pragmatic, results-oriented information processors. It squashes creativity ... except in how to beat the system. One learns only for monetary reward.

And the children who were paid to keep their rooms tidy? What happens when that system doesn't apply? No money, no tidiness.

This is not to say that money is not effective in incentivizing people to work harder and smarter. But there are some serious and important caveats.

Peanut-money managers are right about money being, for some, an incentive, but they need to know how and when money works? We know there are five conditions that need to be met to ensure that any sort of incentive plan works:

1. Employees must value the extra money they will make under the plan. The question is, how much will really make them sit up and take notice? And a problem here is that, for some, it is enough, while for others in the same group or team it is not.
2. The employee must not lose important things/values (health, job security and the like) in striving for high performance. Is the cost of the money worth it? What is the sacrifice for mere money?
3. Employees must be able to control their own performance so that they have a chance to strive further. Is the job designed so that there is a clear and logical relationship between input and output? Who else is involved? This is why it all works reasonably well in sales, because the effort–output ratio is clear. No one in sales believes in luck. They know you make your own luck.
4. The employee must clearly understand how the plan/process works. Make it fiendishly complex or have some small-print caveats and you are finished, and if the worker senses that his/her manager is being dishonest or underhand, the equation is multiplied by zero.

5. It must be possible to measure performance accurately (using indices of performance, cost effectiveness, or ratings) for all those who contribute. This is often the most difficult part. Easy if you are selling widgets, but much more difficult for complex knowledge work.

The trouble with money is that it is too cold and too objective. Just as money is quite unacceptable as a gift, so it is ineffective in the long run as a motivator of people in the workplace.

# Power and status in organizations

"No CEO should be paid more than 10 times the amount that the lowest paid worker in the organization receives." Discuss. Who dares to disagree? Who dares to suggest the education level, stress and workload of top people is often easily 10 times that of their support staff? And what of the consequences of the cock-ups made by an incumbent in the top job versus the most lowly paid worker?

So what about perks, then? Don't the grown-ups have bigger offices, more support staff, designated parking spaces? And is all that not right and proper? 'Twas ever thus. The natural order. We are social animals. We live in tribes. We are led by alpha males – silverbacks who have all the privileges.

In some societies and social groups there is a strong belief in the naturalness, necessity and inevitability of hierarchies. To the people in them it is self-evident that all people are not born equal, and that an efficient organization and society requires a broadly accepted ordering of people. The alternative is chaos and anarchy, which would be much worse than harsh authority. Deferring to authority, respecting tradition and obedience to rule-makers is perceived as beneficial, prudent and upright rather than pusillanimous and weak.

For those national and corporate culture gurus who might be reading this, we are talking about the phenomenon *power-distance*. This means essentially the extent to which less powerful people in a group (company, country or institution) accept the fact that power (and the rewards that it brings) is distributed unequally.

Some organizations are flat, with fewer hierarchies. They tend to be less centralized and the wage differentials are lower. This is often the case with churches. There, the blue-white collar differentials are not as dramatic. The poorest might get 5–8 times less than the richest. Some countries try hard, through taxation and the egalitarian ethic, to reduce differences within organizations. The Australians who snip off the tall poppy, and the high-taxing Scandinavians, believe that less distance and fewer differences lead to greater general well-being. This is the theme of Wilkinson and Pickett's book, *The Spirit Level* (2009).

On the other hand, high-power-distance countries and cultures have no problem with class and caste, or rank and power. They inevitably have a taller pyramid, more levels, more supervisors and a greater centralization. The top and the bottom are miles apart. And, no intervention is necessary in this Darwinian world where the winner takes all and the strong thrive. To him who hath, shall more be given; and the meek do not inherit the earth.

It is not difficult to see the difference between power-tolerant and power-respecting cultures. In the former, children are encouraged by parents who are equals to have a will of their own. But in the latter, children are socialized into obedience by parents who are supervisors. Power-tolerant societies favor student-centered educators and the impersonal learning of truths, while the power-respecting education is teacher-centered and scholars receive "wisdom" from their teachers. Teachers in this mode are jugs filled with wisdom, which they pour into empty vessels. The truths they impart are to be accepted uncritically and even memorized as a sign of definite commitment.

The low-power-distant, power-tolerant workplace sees hierarchies as being there for convenience and efficiency. Subordinates expect to be consulted and listened to, and the ideal boss is a resourceful democrat. High-power-distant corporate cultures accept the benevolent autocrat/godfather boss who expects obedience from subordinates who have been given their orders. Hierarchies reflect inequalities, which are obvious, inevitable and have to be accepted.

People in high-power-distant cultures are more dependent on, and respectful of, their bosses. They tend to be more emotionally distant and feel it is wrong to approach, and particularly to contradict, their bosses. They accept the power and authority of the boss.

People from high-power-distant and power-respecting cultures are easy to insult. Those sensitive to rank can be offended if asked to deal, or even dine, with someone of a lower rank. They don't like the chumminess of low-power-distance, first-name-calling managers. And they do not expect to get their hands dirty, even in an emergency.

The power-tolerant manager may experience the power-sensitive culture as rule-bound, autocratic, inflexible and old-fashioned. Most of all it is perceived as nonegalitarian, discriminatory and deeply unjust – full of "isms": sexism, racism and so on.

The clash of the two opposing cultures is seen in cross-border mergers and acquisitions, in joint ventures, and in expansion into new territories.

Both sides can be deeply shocked and offended by the beliefs and practices of the other.

By and large there is a "fit" between national and corporate cultures. Traditional Scandinavian companies mirror the national culture. And the same is true of Asian and South American cultures. But the world is now a smaller place. And the old West needs young immigrants to supply essential services.

Some organizations have invented ingenious rules to deal with particular problems. In the British army – and uniquely for such a prototypical power-distance organization – padres adopt the rank of the person to whom they are speaking. They are always equal, whether they are addressing a corporal or a colonel; a neat solution to a potentially tricky power-distance problem.

## Reference

Wilkinson, R. and Pickett, K. (2009) *The Spirit Level*. London: Penguin.

# Processes, profit and people

Go through a good MBA class and ask people about their backgrounds. Yes, there will be a number of oddballs, priests and doctors, actors and architects, but these classes are usually dominated by two groups of people – engineers and accountants.

The situation with engineers is so grave in some countries that governments are becoming seriously worried. Supply never meets demand, because soon after qualification – and where necessary paying back their loan – they go to business school to become rich, successful captains of industry.

It's easier to explain the plethora of accountants: they want to widen their perspective and understand the whole business. Accounts give one a very profound idea of how businesses run: profit and loss and all that, but there is a wider picture.

By definition, accountants and engineers have a facility with numbers. They see patterns, do calculations, apply formulae with ease. They favor statistical modelling of problems. They often stride through what are considered to be the hardest parts of the MBA course – that is, finance econometric modelling, and some parts of strategy. They are convinced, and partly rightly, that the key to everything lies in numbers.

Engineers understand business process. They understand how to design systems that lead to efficiency. They know how technology can radically alter the way that things are done, and they appreciate flow models. Hence the fashion a few years ago in business for process reengineering. This seemed to imply that structural issues were of major importance. Critiqued later as a quick-fix, short-term move that simply took out middle management and derailed the company, for a time it enjoyed widespread success.

The sharp eyes of the engineers, and their understanding of how things fit together and operate can be a great asset in business. It is no wonder that the great production-line, time-and-motion people were engineers by training. They also dealt with human factors in the form of man–machine interactions.

Accountants often have the best understanding of the health of a business. This is more than merely reading or drawing up a profit and loss statement. Often, they understand *real* costs, and have a good eye for waste and savings. They also, very usefully, come to know legal issues surrounding tax. They can save companies a fortune by recommending changes that have high tax implications. The best have a good knowledge of finance, stock markets and currency speculation. More than most, they understand global monetary issues and trends.

Both accountants and engineers take to strategy. Indeed, many leave business school to join the great management consultancy firms who often describe themselves as strategy consultants. They offer a careful (in-depth, brilliant, total) analysis of the current state of the organization, and as a result, make recommendations as to what is to be done.

See the  work and thinking of accountants and engineers. It comes (relatively) easily to them. And it's beguiling for the less well-trained. Closely argued and supported by mountains of data and analysis, these "outsiders" appear to understand individual organizations far better than the "insiders" who have worked there for a decade.

But there appears to be something missing in all this: people. When managers are young they believe that problems in the company lie in structures, processes or products, but as they get older they realize that it's *people*. Get a dozen CEOs of small businesses (those with a turnover of £30 million or less) and ask them to list their major ongoing and intransigent problems. They may mention bank loans or leases on buildings, but more often comments are made about individuals. They are less interested in how people tick, however, as in how to solve the problem of particular individuals who are "difficult."

"People people" are often not particularly interested in business *per se*. Of course, this begs the question as to why, how and when they got into business. Certainly, anthropology or psychology degrees guarantee nothing. It may be argued that those arts graduates who read great literature receive a far better insight into the foibles, peccadilloes and capriciousness of people.

In business, those (supposedly) most interested in people issues and welfare are those in employed Human Resources (HR). HR has changed over time, along with the labels they have given themselves. Originally simply called the Staff Department, many now call themselves Talent Management Department or even more simply the People Department. HR departments deal with many issues such as payroll, the Inland Revenue, health and safety and so on.

If the accountants and the engineers look after the other resources (finance, plant, stock, knowledge), then the HR Department looks after the human side of things. Yet, as noted in an earlier essay, comparatively few HR directors sit on the board and few CEOs come from an HR background. Further, the HR Department is almost universally disliked and reviled: and generally thought to be a waste of money.

Perhaps too often HR cannot help the senior managers with the real people issues. Perhaps they do not have the skills or the courage to do so – or the people problems are essentially unsolvable. Perhaps people problems are among the most intractable of all. Perhaps HR have tried to "ape" the engineers and become too obsessed by processes and procedures, and in doing so have forgotten what they were really expected to do.

# Protecting vulnerable customers

Frequently, on those mildly addictive consumer report television programmes, we get reports of unscrupulous people targeting the elderly. The targets tend to have certain things in common: they live alone, they are middle class, and are relatively easily parted from their money. They tend to be trusting, and some appear to have rather a lot of "senior moments."

Old people are, like all of us, sold things by cold callers on the telephone as well as on the doorstep. And they too are told that they have won spectacular prizes that are, of course, bogus. Younger and less-well-educated people with more "street smarts" and "savvy" are generally not potential prey for this growing problem.

The issue of exploiting the vulnerable, or potentially vulnerable, is an issue of increasing importance to governments and regulators. On the one hand, people are living longer. Older people often have fairly large sums of disposable income available. Manufacturers are now interested in providing various expensive gadgets and goods that increase or facilitate mobility (such as stairlifts or electric scooters) as well as products to make things physically more comfortable (special chairs and beds, for example).

On the other hand, with regard to selling through the internet, television and the telephone, current regulations don't offer the vulnerable the same safeguards as they would if these products were bought on the High Street.

And, more interestingly, it's not inconceivable that a vulnerable person could (unwittingly, of course) exploit organizations selling to them; how long before a customer that is subsequently found to be vulnerable takes an organization to court on the basis that they did not put the proper safeguards in place. Often this is done by a relative who feels angry that their kith and kin had been deceived; but it could equally be done by "victims" themselves.

So how to protect the vulnerable? Certainly, this has become the focus of court cases, which will no doubt increase in the future. Various groups have been working on these issues, including myself and a colleague, Thomas Bayne.

Of necessity, one starts with a definition. What does it mean to be vulnerable, as in a customer vulnerable or easily exploited by high-pressure sales techniques?

Being vulnerable means that some people are more susceptible than the average person to the influence of high-pressure salesmen. It is not just the elderly who are their victims. Those people whose first language is not English are just as liable. The definition of vulnerability is an important issue for businesses. It can even be a matter of life or death. A broad definition, and one favored by regulators, would preclude many businesses from reselling to many of the customers they've already sold to, and therefore limit the potential for future growth.

There are two problems with arriving at a straightforward working definition: the first is that vulnerability is clearly a dimension graded from "not at all" to "very," and regulators have the near-impossible task of drawing a pretty simple line in the sand. Next, of course, there are different types of vulnerability. Four can readily be distinguished:

1. *Comprehension vulnerability*: this is essentially about understanding what one is being sold, at what price and under what conditions. It is related to many factors such as education, intelligence, mother tongue, culture and age. Many people claim they did not understand the contract document which they signed, meaning they did not fully or sufficiently comprehend what they were told or sold, and all the subtle and terribly important ramifications of the sale. Indeed, as is known, what the "big print" giveth, the "small print" taketh away.

   Older people have problems with hearing, and with short-term memory. Many may have had little contact with financial language. This problem is compounded if their first language is not (in this case) English, or they come from a culture where the "rules" of selling are very different. This is always compounded by home selling, as there are many complex rules about treating strangers in the home.

   Comprehension vulnerability can be tested for, providing a good study for a psycho-gerentologist or a cognitive psychologist. But we know the groups from which these people are most likely to come and we can devise safeguards that protect them.

2. *Financial vulnerability*: Many people are effectively financially illiterate, irresponsible or troubled. They very easily get into debt by buying on the "never-never." They readily buy things they really cannot afford, and undertake to make regular repayments that they can, in no way, serve.

Many do not understand the arithmetic of interest rates. They may be unwilling, unused to, or unable to save to make better financial arrangements. Further, they may not understand the possibilities of "haggling" for discounts and so on. The financially vulnerable tend to be less educated, though some are fairly well-educated, of course. Such people are often detectable through a history of repossessions or problematic credit records.

3. *Physically vulnerable*: Many people suffer from various forms of sensory or motor impairment. They may not see or hear well, and have difficulty getting about. They may as a consequence be particularly vulnerable in their own homes, where they feel unable to eject people.

   Physical vulnerability naturally links to comprehension vulnerability. And it increases with age. Essentially, the issue is that one or more disabilities affects a person's ability to make reasonable decisions. They can't fully inspect goods; they can't read the small print; they do not hear all the information they are being given.

4. *Assertiveness vulnerability*: This concerns having the social skills associated with negotiating. It means feeling comfortable and confident in simply saying "no" without shame, embarrassment or incoherence.

   There are countless cases of people buying things they really didn't want because they didn't know how to turn away an experienced and subtle salesperson who fully understands how to manipulate emotions.

There may be other types of vulnerability, or other words to describe it, but the above categories seem to capture most of the issues. Of course, they are all related, and some groups may be particularly vulnerable.

However, it is no doubt that it is the first vulnerability – comprehension – that is the most fundamental. It is also where good companies and the law can intervene.

So, how can you make sure you are not abusing the comprehension vulnerable by selling them something they may have wanted but did not understand the cost and conditions and consequences of the contract? It's not practical to give them an intelligence, hearing or credit-worthiness test.

But there are things organizations who sell to potentially vulnerable customers can and should do. First, consider the selling situation. Where is the transaction taking place, what are the social norms and conventions, how much pressure is being brought to bear on the individual? The dentist's chair may be a good example of a place where it is harder to make good decisions.

But there are sensible and sensitive checks and balance that can be put in place relatively easily when booking or confirming a sales appointment. This provides an excellent opportunity to ask a few unobtrusive questions, which may help to identify the comprehension vulnerable. They are, of course, not as crude as the famous sectioning questions such as "What day is it today?" or "Who is the prime minister?"

One can, to some extent, hear if someone is deaf, or confused or a non-native speaker struggling with the language. But sometimes basic questions can tap into memory and understanding. What is the nearest main road or main line station? What is your full postcode? Have you ever bought any of these (or similar) products before? What day of the week were you born on? The dates of the births of their spouse or children, or of the date of their wedding?

What organizations could do when going through a relatively well-thought-through and tested script is to ensure that they are categorizing potential customers in terms of their risk of being comprehension vulnerable. This could be, say, graded on a three- or five-point scale from "not at all," through "potentially" to "very."

Any sales person or organization needs to size up its appetite for risk at this point. Risks of court cases, loss of reputation, risks of default in repayments and so on. It is far better to have a well-thought-through plan and strategy to avoid the vulnerable consumer and to manage those who are potentially vulnerable. This may mean asking for a friend or relative to be present at the sales meeting.

It certainly would be a paradox if companies that do not take full cognisance of the vulnerability of their customers end up themselves being highly vulnerable in the eyes of the law.

# Quant Jocks and qual Jills

The commercially minded (read avaricious), moderately socially skilled (read can do small talk), really smart (read brilliant) "quant Jocks" earn fortunes. They are masters of the universe: the kings of the jungle.

City firms are hungry for Ph.D. Maths, Physics and Engineering people who are extremely numerate. All those brilliant algorithms, computer models and technical breakthroughs are the products of these quick-as-lightning, deductive thinkers. Some with a taste for fame and inventions discover the commercial side of their talents while still undergraduates, while others stay in the safe cloisters of the university until hunger drives them into the warm, even hot, embrace of commercial life.

Google, Facebook, Microsoft and a host of others are the "brainchildren" of quant Jocks. Many with less entrepreneurial charm can still do very well tumbling the tough numbers in the City. Their gift, often discovered relatively early in life, has helped them to sail through school and university with nothing but the very top grades. They make mincemeat of physics, maths, extra maths, advanced maths and statistics. Some also excel in music and other code-breaking subjects. They don't write well or enjoy literature much as a rule. Many have a thinly disguised contempt for "social science."

Jealousy and envy, often disguised in left-wing, politically-correct talk, have led sometimes to attempted revenge on these superstar quant Jocks. They are described as inadequate nerds, geeks or techies who can't do social interaction, establish relationships or appreciate emotional work. Cognitive intelligence max score, emotional intelligence nil.

They are supposed to have no people skills. It is assumed that they think persuasion is all about winning the argument, having more data or smarter analysis, and think management is about having a clever plan and giving orders. And they are perplexed by the capriciousness of people's emotions, particularly those of the opposite sex.

The emotional intelligence fraternity, without a scrap of evidence, trumpeted the idea that emotional intelligence is "more important" than intelligence at work. And they echoed that same idea in claiming that we are *all intelligent* in different ways. A sop to the dim and talentless. They assert that such things as kinaesthetic, spiritual and existential intelligence are important at work, more so than the ability to add up, do accounts and read balance sheets. Evidence-free tosh, but that doesn't stop the gurus writing books to the contrary.

But the rich, powerful, quant Jocks can take it. Some even rejoice in their image. They know the power of numbers and the need for their skills. No need to waste energy on those who are less talented.

There is another group, called the "qual people." Market researchers talk of the importance of quant and qual. And it is true that qual people tend more often to be women. They do focus groups and in-depth interviews. They try to read between the lines, or get under the surface to discover what people are trying to say, or really mean.

The output of the qual person is usually a wordy report with some "sexy," journalistic-type quotes. Indeed, qual research is often about finding and describing different personality types and emotions. But these are little more than typologies: putting people in boxes with amusing sound titles. There is little discussion about the relationship between the boxes, or any description of how they got there. It is categorical, not dimensional.

Some "qual Jills" rejoice in their reputation for having a "third eye," a "super-tuned ear," a way of understanding the motives, hopes and ambitions of people who don't even understand themselves. They are the psychoanalysts of the market place. But like psychoanalysis, their ideas are difficult to refute or test.

Qual Jills have claimed to be experts in areas such as non-verbal communication, or followers of the very unacademic neurolinguistic programming (NLP). They are supposed to be brilliant communicators, but some, as they become more successful, seem to be permanently on "transmit" and never receive.

There is indeed a theory for this observable difference, called the essential difference between the sexes. Women are better at emotions and empathizing, while men are better at things/objects and systematizing.

Empathizing is the ability to identify another person's emotions and thoughts, and to respond to them with an appropriate emotion. It helps in understanding another person, in predicting their behavior, and connecting or resonating with their feelings. It is about naturally and spontaneously tuning into the other person's thoughts and feelings, whatever these might be. Empathizers read others well and know how to deal with and manage their own and others' emotions.

Systematizing is the ability to analyze and explore things, and construct a system or theory for how they work. The systematizer is good at understanding how things work. He or she is compelled to extract the underlying rules that govern the behavior of a system. This is done in order to understand and predict the mechanisms ("where the wires go") and, where appropriate, to invent new ones.

The theory of the well-known psychologist, Simon Baron-Cohen, is that males, on the whole, have stronger abilities to systematize, and females greater abilities in empathizing: "He has an S-brain, and she an E-brain." Quant Jocks and qual Jills in the workplace are a reflection of this fundamental difference.

# Recognition programs that don't work

Reward recognition at work is a very important but rather tricky business. Most employers want intrinsically motivated people who don't need too much extrinsic reward (read money). But there's a whole raft of ideas on how to reward good performance, apart from money or time.

Staff can join exclusive clubs such as the Talent Group, or even be allowed to become a mentor of younger people, though some may see this more as a punishment than a reward. They could become 5-star generals, as McDonald's used to have, showing customers how experienced and the expert staff were. Special uniforms work quite well in some environments, as do fancy (if meaningless) titles.

One idea widely used in the service sector is "Employee of the Month" (EOM). It is not uncommon anywhere in the world to find some surprised or scowling person from housekeeping or the kitchen staring out from a cheap photograph in the lobby. He or she is the employee of the month: an exemplar of the service that is required.

The concept is that this gives just credit to deserving individuals, boosts morale through symbolic rewards and motivates excellence by providing positive examples for other employees to emulate. There are questions about who nominates the employee of the month: customers, supervisors or managers? Possibly some combination of these. And what are they rating? A one-off encounter over a meal, a week-long interaction as a room-steward, or what?

Hotel and airline customers are usually aware of how often they are asked to rate the service provided. Bedrooms and bars, dining rooms and health spas, all have little cards requiring ratings. On airlines your questionnaire has often been preset by a random process designed to improve sampling. Many of the forms ask you to nominate a person who has provided exemplary service or who has "has delighted you". This is usually part of the data for EOM systems.

These systems have their problems. Indeed, it is possible that they will backfire, causing the many non-awardees to be increasingly demotivated. There are four issues here. The *first* is the *means to the end*. It is not beyond belief to expect that some employees engage in undesirable, unethical or even illegal behaviors to get the result they want. They may fake guest feedback cards, or attempt to bully their peers.

A *second* problem is the *front of house/back of house* issue. It's the problem of tips in restaurants: should the waiter/waitress receive the money as the client intended, or should it be shared by the other more skilful and important people who are out of sight, such as the cook. How, in a hotel, does the laundry manager receive the prize of EOM? This means customer ratings alone cannot suffice as the data bank.

A *third* problem is that the *behavioral criteria* for earning the EOM are unclear. One study asked employees to specify what they had to do to become the EOM and none could do so. It all seems too capricious and not prescriptive enough. The cynical but ambitious worker may target particular customers likely to be docile, undemanding and happy to make the necessary recommendation.

*Fourth*, it's a *winner takes all* system. The vast majority of people are not rewarded, despite there being an almost indistinguishable difference between their behaviors. It's a "first past of the post" problem.

These norm-based systems mean that reward is not based only on an individual's own merit but also that of others. Thus making others look bad makes an individual look comparatively good. In which case, talented, hard-working, dedicated individuals may never be rewarded because others are (slightly) more so. This can lead people to ideas about the covert sabotage of peers.

*Fifth*, if EOM systems *are* truly based on performance, then it would be very likely that the same individual would win very regularly, indeed almost all the time. This would prevent people from ever being an EOM, which paradoxically extinguishes (as the behaviorists say) the very desirable behaviors managers are trying to encourage. This problem is often approached by ruling that people can only be an EOM once, or once a year.

But this can backfire, because it becomes a "Buggin's turn" game based on nothing but tedious turn-taking. This is quite unrelated to good service but is a rather pointless activity where people wait in line for a small, almost humiliating reward. The problem is that, intuitively for many, if you are not a winner you are by definition a loser.

Proponents of these systems use sporting analogies. Those who aren't nominated as the EOM will be motivated to try harder. Nonsense, say opponents – if anything, it makes people angry, apathetic and interested in sabotage. Indeed, the reward for EOM maybe the ability to make all your colleagues look less efficient and less helpful than yourself.

One recent study by Johnson and Dickinson (2010) put some of these ideas to the test. And they found exactly what they had expected: EOMs backfire and have the effect of doing the opposite to what was intended: that is, they lower staff morale overall.

So it's back to the drawing board to find a cheap and effective way to motivate customer-facing staff.

## Reference

Johnson, D. and Dickinson, A. (2010) "Employee-of the-Month Programs," *Journal of Organizational Behavior Management*, 30: 308–24.

# Religion at work

Would you be more or less inclined to hire a person if you knew he or she was strongly religious? Would it really depend on what religion it was? Are those who are evangelical, "strict" or fanatical much the same in their attitudes, beliefs and behaviors? Are you engaging a person of moral integrity or blind intolerance; a person of compassion or inflexibility? Are converts more dangerous than those "born into the faith?" How does religion have an impact on behavior at work?

Religion is clearly a "no-no" at work. Religious discrimination is quite clearly and rightly illegal. But discrimination over *religiousness* is not. It is the difference between being a believer and being a believer in a very particular deity, set of deities or scriptural revelation. It is not illegal to ask people if they are religious, but it certainly is to ask about their particular faith. Religious is not the same as spiritual. Religiousness is usually thought of as a set of shared beliefs and behaviors associated with this life and the afterlife, good and evil, the meaning of life. For most people this implies observance of certain behavioral traditions associated with food, dress or worship as well as a range of metaphysical beliefs.

Certainly religion is widely discussed today. The irreverent challenges the Right Reverend; the atheist the theist; and the cynical and sceptical challenges the accepting and believing. There is a big debate about faith schools and the power of religion for good and evil in the world. Religions compete as they have always done, but now they are up against highly articulate, militant atheists.

At work, the biggest issue appears to be the wearing of religious symbols. Employers worry about demands for prayer rooms or prayer breaks; fetishism in the canteen; and demands for holidays on holy days. Managers are concerned about the "genie-in-the-bottle" phenomenon. Let one group have "special privileges" and everybody wants some. So it's best to brush the whole thing under the carpet.

Thus the topic remains taboo. The shadow of litigation, boycotts and even arson or Luddism hangs over the bewildered manager in post-Christian, crypto-materialistic Britain. But the question is what to expect of a highly religious person at work. Clearly, there may be polarized views.

The negative view might encompass the idea of intolerance, dogmatism and rigidity. Some argue that there is evidence that less intelligent and less educated people are the most religious, and that religious people are less able and agile in decision-making. Bloody-mindedness always trumps compromise, and traditionalism is the enemy of adaptation, change and development.

Those critical of religion have always noted the often stark contrast between the messages of peace, inclusiveness and self-sacrifice, and behaviors associated with aggression, discrimination and a zeal for the ostracism or humiliation of those not of the (one true) faith.

The positive view may place stress on the reliability and morality of the religious persona at work. Over 100 years ago, the German economist and sociologist, Max Weber, proposed the view, in contrast to Karl Marx, that it was religious forces (namely European Protestantism) that led to the development of capitalism. The Protestant Ethic hypothesis was that the stress on work being in itself a good (and godly) thing; the stress on asceticism and rationality; and the (extraordinary) belief that wealth was a sign of grace led to the development of wealthy, democratic capitalist countries.

The debate is now a century old and multidisciplinary. People with a strong work ethic tend to be achievement oriented. They want to get on with people at work but also to move ahead of them. They favor equity over equality and they are competitive.

One of the great values of the original Protestant Ethic was its emphasis on rationality and a rejection of the mumbo-jumbo of Catholic sacramentalism. It also rejected all intermediaries (bishops, priests, deacons, saints, angels and the like) between oneself and the Almighty.

A strong Protestant childhood leads to respect for rationality and science, a belief in the postponement of gratification, of saving and wise time management. The values of sport are the values of Protestantism: extensive practice, winner takes all, competitiveness. It could be argued that Islamic or Jewish work ethics share the same values.

The work ethic view is that religion often makes better workers. People who pitch up and pitch in. Honest, reliable, trustworthy workers: salt of the earth. Those who require minimal supervision because they are guided from within to follow rules, do their duty and respect their fellow humans.

Volunteers often tend to be religious. As are charity givers – but it is mainly to people of their own faith. The worry for people at work is that religion is a litmus paper for the malcontent. Most would prefer employees keep their faith to themselves, to be followed as an after-work activity.

But religious people believe they cannot compartmentalize their lives so conveniently: they are obliged to speak up and act out their faith everywhere and all the time.

So, another example of the poor employers who are damned if they do and damned if they don't. Unless, of course, they are an institution with a very clear religious affiliation, such as a Christian radio station, a Muslim bank, or a Baptist university.

## Reference

Therivel, W. (1999) "Why Are Eccentrics Not Eminently Creative?," *Creativity Research Journal*, 12, 47–55.

# Resilience and hardiness

Do you recall the "Brown bounce" that didn't happen? The British ex-prime minister was meant to bounce back and jump-start the hopes of the Labour Party. Ultimately, however, he did more to seal its fate than increase its fortunes.

But the ability to bounce back is crucial in business. Leadership is tough, stressful and energy-draining. Amen. There is the unpredictable around every corner. Events on the far side of the world have profound effects. People let you down. Suppliers and customers go bust. Inflation, deflation, stealth taxes ... and so on.

No wonder emotional stability or adjustment is such an important predictor of managerial success. It's all about coping with adversity. And it is an important issue to explore at selection time. Here is a good question: "Describe the greatest adversity you have experienced and say how you (and others) reacted to it." Listen to how serious the event was, how it was described, and what the candidate did to solve the problem. As a follow-up question, ask the interviewees what they learned from the experience.

In a theory about creativity, a psychologist called William Therivel devised a concept called the *GAM theory*. The G stands for genetic endowment, without which, almost by definition, genius is not possible. The A stands for the assistance of youth, and the M for misfortune. He wrote one paper with the memorable title of "Why Mozart and not Salieri?" His thesis, backed up by good scholarship, was that recovering from major adversity, with assistance, was a factor in the flowering of genius. If you had the "genetic endowment" and if you were helped, you could come through all sorts of misfortune. And having done so, nothing can scare or trouble you quite as much again. It establishes and enhances resilience.

Without doubt, the worst thing that can happen to a child is the loss of a parent. Death is sometimes worse than divorce, though the latter can have a powerful impact on the attachment pattern of the child toward the parent with whom they live.

The loss of the parent can mean the loss of security, of predictability, of safety. Your guide, your protector, your major source of all types of support is gone. The sky darkens, and the future becomes unclear. There are those who can help in this crisis: the other parent, relatives, friends. Some may provide, in time, a good substitute for the missing parent.

Such adversity can make or break people. If you can survive this crisis then nearly everything else pales into insignificance. If you know you have been through the darkest night of the soul and survived, other problems are more easily put into perspective.

Children who have been parachuted into half a dozen different schools because of their parents' geographical wanderings learn to cope: to make friends, to join groups, to blend in. Boarding-school children learn self-sufficiency, as do foreign students.

Adversity does not have to be traumatic, though it can be. Some, as the advertisements say, do make a drama out of a crisis, and others a crisis out of an upset. And some are blessed enough to be able to see things for what they are, and deal with them appropriately.

Some people appear to be more resilient than others. They bounce back and pick themselves up after falling. They seem hardier; but not callous or selfish, or cynical. They are not easily fazed by the "slings and arrows of outrageous fortune."

Resilient people have to been studied to try to understand their dynamics. First, they seem to have a deep sense of involvement or commitment to all aspects of their life: work, home, friends, family, and they are socially well connected. Indeed, this is one of their protective factors. They seem to have a number of important, central and secure relationships. They are not alienated and isolated. They are networked. They care, and are cared for, both at home and at work.

Next, they tend to see setbacks and problems as challenges and puzzles rather than insurmountable hurdles or obstacles. They are more likely to see these events as interesting opportunities for growth rather than stressful, threatening and anxiety-provoking events. It's more than an optimistic versus a pessimistic outlook, but is related to these.

Challenges impose demands on resources. They stretch you but don't break you. More than that, they can provide opportunities to learn, change and grow. Just as pain therapists encourage patients to redefine the way they describe their feelings, so resilient and hardy people have learned to think about adversity differently. The resilient learn lessons: what to do and what not. And therefore how to cope better next time, for surely, with many adversities, there is indeed a next time.

Third, hardy and resilient people know well the dangers of fatalism and helplessness. They tend to have a sense of personal control: the belief that they can influence their life outcomes. There are things they can do to increase their well-being. They are not victims of chance, fate or powerful, dark and capricious forces that control their lives. As a consequence, they try and usually succeed in improving their lot.

So check out resilience in a potential employee. Listen to how he or she talks and think about the issues. Don't underestimate the manager who can cope with stress.

# Resistance to change

Some call it change; others progress; some adaptation. Some people are clearly change-phobic, while others are change-lovers. The former prefer steady-as-you-go predictability and doing things in the old way, but change-lovers adore the new, the different and anything that is state-of-the-art.

Those who love change usually prefer to change structures, processes or systems rather than people. They might be advocates of organizational learning or change management. But there are those who are committed to changing people though training, coaching and mentoring, but they prefer words like learning and development.

Change is inevitable; and it's happening faster than ever these days. We are told, "If you don't change, you die." Heard it all before … and it is very gratifying when some daft, pointless initiative is introduced then quietly removed from the workplace after the inevitable law of unintended consequences snaps into action. And perhaps all that change talk is little more than a plot to keep expensive consultants – pretentiously called "change agents" – from fleecing the company.

Certainly, some organizations change more quickly, dramatically and easily than others. As an example, compare Apple with the Roman Catholic Church. Obviously, it has something to do with their product, their culture and, most important, their competition.

We all personally know the great difficulty of change. Breaking or changing habits is extremely difficult to do, even if it does not involve addictive substances such as nicotine. Diets don't work because they don't involve permanent change.

But there are clearly individual differences or dispositional factors associated with change. Some people seem to embrace change, indeed thrive on it, much more than others. The young seem happier to change than the old, no doubt because they have fewer habitual responses, or less to lose.

It's not clear whether intelligence and education affect a person's attitudes to and embracing of change. Certainly it is a reasonable assumption that brighter people should fear learning new things less and see when necessary change must occur. But they can also mount an impressive casuistic and sophistic response to it.

And what about gender and culture? Do the relatively powerless react to change rather differently from those in control? Do cultures with fatalistic religions and values go with the flow more happily than those that emphasize personal responsibility and control?

Psychologists have found several personality factors that they believe relate to change:

1. *Neuroticism/adjustment.* Those labelled as neurotic are prone to anxiety and depression; they see danger everywhere; and they are hypervigilant for possible threats. To survive the stressful workplace they need manifold and effective coping strategies. Change inevitably stresses them because they worry about what it means, what they need to do and learn, and how they will cope. The resistant, hardy and stable personalities do better.
2. *Self-efficacy and control.* Some people believe they are captains of their own ship, masters of their fate. They (largely) control their destiny and they are personally efficacious. They are contrasted with fatalists, who believe that chance, fate and powerful others influence everything. Those who believe they have control exercise it and cope better.
3. *Tolerance of ambiguity.* Some people feel significantly threatened by lack of clarity and uncertainty. They like things to be open, clear, predictable and orderly. Even in a capricious, unstable work environment they strive to avoid uncertainty through the use of rules, regulation and rituals that dictate behavior: the more comfortable people are around ambiguity, the easier it is for them to accept and embrace change.

Recently, two Israeli psychologists have been working on a simple measure of personal resistance to change (see Shaul and Sverdik 2011). They found four factors that predicted an individual's resistance to (imposed) change at work. These were:

- *Routine-seeking.* Many people like a stable routine. They would rather be bored than surprised. They take comfort in their little daily rituals which change threatens to destabilize.
- *Stress and tension.* Any threat to stability can make some individuals experience great discomfort. Any change at work can signal danger, which leads to worry which in turn can, in time, lead to a drop in performance. And this could necessitate more change.

- *Short-term thinking.* Here, people focus on immediate inconvenience and discomfort, even if they are aware of long-term benefits; it's the "jam today" response. Such a short-term focus is somewhat irrational.
- *Cognitive rigidity.* This used to be called dogmatism and was used pejoratively. It is a profound dislike of changing one's mind and view.

Most people are (quite rightly) ambivalent about change. Much depends on one's experience of change and the extent to which it is imposed from above. Equally, possibly even more important, is the person's attitude to the "change agent" – usually senior management. The worst combination is having someone dispositionally resistant to change who also fundamentally distrusts the change agent. But if the messenger is trusted then even the most change-phobic person will go along with the new rules and regulations.

The moral of the story? Target the resistors of change; work on them and gain their trust.

## Reference

Shaul, O. and Sverdik, N. (2011) "Ambivalence toward Imposed Change: The Conflict between Dispositional Resistance to Change and the Orientation toward the Change Agent," *Journal of Applied Psychology*, 96: 337–49.

# The scientific understanding of the public

The most famous atheist of our time, Richard Dawkins, held a chair in the Public Understanding of Science. Others have copied this clever idea, so there are Professors of the Public Understanding of Psychiatry, one of Psychology, and one of the Media. It's all about determining the public's lamentable knowledge about a topic and then providing education on the subject.

It is not difficult to demonstrate the public's ignorance, prejudice and stereotypic beliefs about any subject, from how things (the body, cars, medicine) work to a knowledge of the past. Media "vox pop" interviews show how inarticulate and bewildered so many people appear to be when faced with direct knowledge questions. Television programmes even show how 10-year-olds often know a lot more than supposedly sophisticated adults.

This is perhaps why there are so many charities, often started as self-help or support groups, whose task, as they see it, is to better inform the public about an issue, often a mental illness or handicap. They tend to follow a pattern: first, the shocking statistic about how many there are who suffer from the problem; second, how many famous people have (or have had) it; third, how much they can, have and will achieve, as a function of their problem; and finally, how people can help. They may have a quiz showing how wrong people are in their current assumptions about the affliction.

The research endeavor is all aimed at education. Hence the borrowing of the much-used concept of "*literacy*." So we have economic literacy and media literacy. The former is understanding how business and money work; and the latter how to critique the media. Psychiatric literacy is about understanding the cause, manifestation and treatment of mental illness. Can you spot a psychopath at work? Do you know when your partner is depressed? What does someone with a bipolar disorder look like?

One fun activity is to develop a psychographic typology of the public. It's a favorite journalistic ploy: come up with amusing types graphically illustrated by a cartoonist. People are classified by age, class, sex, region, religion and so on. Good column, but often bad science. But the message is an important one: "the public" is not a single entity.

Then there is a totally different group of researchers. They are not so much interested in what the public knows, but rather about what they *do*. The aim is to influence people's behavior. This is the *scientific understanding of the public*. Such researchers used to be housed in the Ministry of Propaganda. It was these people who were responsible for the most tedious of all announcements and advertisements, namely *public service announcements*.

Yet still at the heart of sales and marketing is the attempt to understand people's behavior. A scientific understanding? Perhaps a social science understanding – sort of "science lite." Marketing is about persuasion. It is an attempt to persuade the public to remember, to buy or to switch brands. The question is, how to do it?

Social scientists argue that there are really only six different, identifiable means of persuading people. These include such things as activating the reciprocity norm (giving free gifts) as well as noting the scarcity of things (last offer, closing down sale, limited edition). These are well known, and used by advertisers who hope to understand and persuade (dare one say manipulate?) the public.

Does the old joke, "About half of all advertising works, but no one knows which half", still apply? Not so much. There are a number of established facts in the world of advertising and marketing. Some techniques work better than others. Amen. The problem lies in all these funny awards that arty types give each other. Like bored theatre critics who have seen *Hamlet* a hundred times and love the nude version set in a 50s theme park, advertisements are often commended for their dramatic impact, use of sound, color or surprise. In many it is not even clear what is being advertised.

But it is not only sales and marketing that need a good shot of social science. More than anyone, it should be Human Resources. They, after all, advise about selection and pay. They demand appraisals and exit interviews. Required processes stream from them, restricting, taxing and frustrating staff at every turn. The question is the evidence base. Is it based on the scientific understanding of the worker? Well, partly.

And what about senior managers, who are meant to lead and inspire teams to achieve strategic goals? We know people need stretching goals and targets, feedback on how they are doing and support. We can increase the specificity of each of these factors – the clarity of goals; the timing and exact nature of feedback; informational and emotional support. We can even say how different individuals in various jobs may react differently. So is this taught in the mushrooming MBAs?

Surely this is all common sense: the sort of thing a "good chap" picks up early in life? Call it emotional intelligence or people skills if you must: is it anything more than charm or a decent amount of insightfulness? Clearly ... and it may account for why so many managers fail and derail.

# Seven lessons for appraisal

Yes, it's true that *everybody* hates the appraisal process. Well, except those who invented it, we assume. All those forms. The bullying HR people demanding that they are completed in a particular way at a particular time. So, often appraiser and appraisee conspire to fulfill the letter, but not the spirit, of the law. It is a bureaucratic chore, not a meaningful process. Paradoxically, what has been designed to improve management only makes it worse, and it gives both management and HR a bad name.

But all staff need feedback and support. It seems inconceivable that someone can be properly managed in that they are not set reasonable, clear and stretching targets, and given the means to achieve them. And it should not be difficult to run a 45-minute interview where the employee is shown how their performance during the year has been rated. But first some tips:

## The Don'ts

1. Don't turn the appraisal into a negotiation exercise by encouraging the employee to rate the form first and then spend the rest of the time comparing scores. This is a recipe for mediocrity: literally. To be appraised means to be evaluated and rated. People are judged in competitions and on the sports field. We do not query the umpire. Imagine at the Olympic Games, going up to the judges afterwards and saying "Well I think I deserve a 9; you only gave me a 7, so let's discuss this." There is a time and place for manager and employee to check each other's perceptions, understandings and ratings. You, the manager, rate the performance of your staff: in ink, not negotiable. Your judgment. By all means use "don't know" or "not applicable," but don't cave in to the evergrowing "demand for a remark" philosophy.

2. Don't be tempted to use words instead of numbers. Words are slippery. What does "satisfactory performance" mean? Allow people to write short descriptions ("must try harder") if they wish, but don't let these replace the precision of numbers. We don't want to encourage semantic debate and discussion: 3/5 is better than 2/5, but it is less clear whether "sustained performance" is better than "consistent work."

3. Don't limit yourself to a 5-point rating scale just because you can't think of more than five words to describe performance: poor, satisfactory, good, excellent, superb. No one uses the bottom number and few the

top, so five points become three points and then there is quite simply no discrimination and differentiation. Have the scales wide and even (like the gates of hell). Anchor each end: *Unacceptable performance* 1 2 3 4 5 6 7 8 9 10 *Superb performance.* You don't need complicated behavioral descriptors of what a 4 looks like or a 9, any more than an Olympic judge does. If the rated behavior is relevant and clear (and it should be), that is enough.

4.  Don't spend any time justifying low marks when showing people their final appraisal form. All that leads to is an argument about the past and a dispute about interpretation. Be able to describe in detail the behavior you want, not the behavior that you don't. Look forward, not back: be descriptive, not evaluative. Tell the appraisee in clear behavioral terms what you want to see and what will merit a high score.

### The Do's

1.  Have a plan. Never hold an (appraisal) meeting without an agenda. And a shared agenda at that. Tell the appraisee before the meeting what you intend to discuss and then find out from them what they want to discuss. Also make sure it is an open, as opposed to hidden, agenda. This is your map. And clarify before the meeting that you understand their agenda points and, more important, that they are relevant to the meeting. Various points the appraisee might want to discuss may be important but are not strictly about performance. The meeting is about the individual performance and the future. And be willing to decode what appraisees are trying to say to you: often they beat about the bush with respect to such things as promotion, pay increases and the like.

2.  At the end of the meeting get the appraisee to summarize the main points raised. This is to check their understanding and to evaluate what they are "taking away." Doctors are trained to do this with patients; it is standard good practice. They should be warned at the beginning of the meeting that they will need to do this, and for most it is not a big deal. Listen carefully to what they say (and don't say). They will repeat what is important to them.

3.  Spend as much time explaining to people what they are doing right as what they are doing wrong. If people have done a good job, spend some time not only thanking and praising them, but also explaining what it is they are doing well. Tell someone their talk was good, say, and they

will probably be pleased, but they can only repeat the performance if they knew what went well: the pace, the jokes, the stories, the slides.

There is no magic bullet for getting appraisals right. But there are simple things one can do. And recall always the warning of Margaret Thatcher when some call for the abolition of the whole thing – "There Is No Alternative."

# Showing off the CEO

Why do all modern prime ministers and elected heads of state have to be seen out jogging? It may have started with US president Jimmy Carter. British prime minister Gordon Brown seems to have got away without doing it. The next best photo opportunity is to play soccer with some kids. Or at least to do some sort of exercise to demonstrate physical fitness.

Consider the images we have of our top people as approved by the PR police. Jogging, playing or (least best) watching sport; greeting all sorts of people, particularly children, heads of state and deprived minorities; receiving rapturous applause from adoring (voting) fans; or working hard in wonderful, exotic foreign environments, thus reflecting their status.

They must be serious and sombre when the occasion requires (Armistice Day); but chummy and jocular the next minute (on "popular" TV programs).

If they are seen eating or drinking it must be tea, not wine. No smoking, no sweating. Hence all the excitement about Nick Clegg, the secret smoker, never caught on camera. They must always look alert, never as if they are dropping off to sleep. They must have a happy, healthy, perfect family. And they must be expensively dressed, as befits their successful states.

Think of the memorable times when leaders got it wrong: in Britain Neil Kinnock stumbling on the beach, and Michael Foot in his donkey jacket. These were not verbal gaffes, though there have been plenty of those: in the US President George W. Bush was in a league of his own: and in articulate John Prescott a poor second on this one.

The PR gurus from the "Ministry of Propaganda" are in direct conflict with the paparazzi and gossip journalists who seek out shots of celebrities being "tired and emotional," "engaging in Ugandan affairs," nodding off during crucial speeches, or falling over. They believe it is their main job to puncture the pomposity of narcissistic CEOs and politicians by showing them as they really are. And rightly so?

But do we really vote for people on the basis of things so trivial or ephemeral? Is there a physiology of leadership: physical requirements to get and hold on to the job?

Evolutionary psychologists say women essentially look for three things in a male mate. You can see these clearly demonstrated in the way males market themselves in lonely-hearts advertisements. Women want physically fit, socially skillful, affluent men: because, as the theory goes, if they are to "make babies" with them they want those infants to be strong, healthy and successful.

We are naked apes. We need alpha males to protect and lead us. Fit, strong, aggressive leaders to protect us from invasion by outsiders. Good leaders ensure the group's survival. They are *clearly dominant*. The Russian prime minister, Vladimir Putin, understands this. Hence the photos showing his bare torso, and his serious scowl. The French President, Nicolas Sarkozy, struggles with his height, being vertically challenged.

Fitness is health and growth. Note how close-up photographs focus on the issue of aging now, as much in men as women. It can be quite odd to see an important figure close up without their TV make-up and back lighting. They seem shorter, less imposing, more ordinary. And that just won't do!

Men signal their social intelligence by their good sense of humor (GSOH). That's social and emotional intelligence. Social skills, charm, charisma – essential for all leadership positions. Social intelligence is, of course, related to real intelligence, which is attractive because it signals career success, money and security.

That easy charm and social confidence is a must, but it must not spill over into arrogance or narcissism. The clothing worn must not be too racy, fashionable or modern. And no patronizing of people, however stupid they apparently are ... except, of course, in debate, where one is expected to show sparkling wit and repartee.

One problem in image-making is money. Rich men are attractive. In some cultures it is acceptable if leaders come from privileged backgrounds and have already made a lot of money. Not so in the West. Perhaps it is OK to have the potential to make money as soon as a leader leaves office. Former prime minister Tony Blair certainly understood this. Leadership positions make you rich.

But a real issue seems to be in the presentation of a female CEO, president or leader. They don't have to jog or do sport. Kissing babies is rather beneath them. And evolutionary psychology will not help here. It's all physical, you see: the male choice of the female is all about shape and sexiness.

Consider Angela Merkel, the German chancellor, Sarah Palin, the former governor of Alaska, or Julia Gillard, the Australian prime minister. How do the marketing and PR people advise them? Not too feminine, lest they seem less powerful? Not too warm, lest they seem less determined? And so on.

The myth of the make-over of Baroness Thatcher was about the hair, the voice and the head movements. She came across originally as too strong and strident; not caring or compassionate enough. So the "helmet" was replaced by big hair, the voice "lowered" and the head encouraged to lean sideways to show attentive listening.

Does all this PR stuff work? You bet it does. Elections are won or lost on small, not big things. It's the medium, not the message, and how, not so much what, things are said.

# Smarts

Since the 1980s, the emotional intelligence gurus have told us that EI is more important/useful/relevant than real intelligence (cognitive ability) at work. They are wrong. And no amount of assertion or anecdote can refute the evidence.

Smarter, brighter, cleverer people do better at work. Intelligence unlocks the doors of education, which gives the knowledge and skills to acquire jobs. Certainly, soft skills help. But they count for little without the horsepower of intelligence.

Emotional intelligence is, quite simply, an astute awareness of one's own and others' emotions: where they come from, how they are manifest, and what triggers them. But, more important, it is about emotional management: the ability to regulate and control emotions to suit the situation. And crucially, at work it is about managing others' emotions, particularly the more negative ones. It is about inspiring the downhearted, dissipating anger and calming fears. Important skills, certainly, but little to do with real intelligence.

Overall, brighter people do better at work. They climb further and faster. They are paid more. And they often enjoy the acclaim, respect and support of others. But there are a few exceptions to the rule: the less bright, very average, mediocre person who really makes it; and the very clever person who becomes an also-ran. The latter are more common than the former, as studies following gifted children have shown.

How is it that averagely (never below average) intelligent people can do well? There are essentially three reasons. *First*, some jobs do not seem to be very clearly related to success; sales is one example. Salespeople have to be motivated and resilient rather than bright to be successful. And many entrepreneurs are self-confessedly not that clever. Spotting opportunities, and having energy and determination are more important. And some entrepreneurs are very, very rich ... and have a very high profile.

*Second*, some people can "inherit" jobs that are far above their ability level. Nepotism remains rife in many organizations, and people can be "gifted" jobs by family members, friends or ideological supporters. Given a job with a good structure and plenty of support, they can appear to do well.

*Third*, while "the Peter Principle" asserts that most people are promoted to their level of incompetence, there are situations in which that incompetence is never fully revealed. Working for a monopoly or an organization where output at an individual or group level is never measured means that those who are pretty average never really get found out.

But what the intellectually unremarkable who make it to the top all have in common is (of necessity) considerable motivation and excellent social skills. They have to persuade by charm rather than through analysis. They have to enlist considerable support for those areas in which they don't do well by themselves. And many have to work very hard to maintain their position.

Most people recognize the never-promoted manager. They have manifold and worrying shortcomings. They tend to be slow and change-averse. Many micro-manage, choosing in effect to work at one or more levels down, where they are more confident and comfortable. Some become rather dependent on their team and are then easy prey for manipulative workers with bigger brains.

But what of the super-smart who don't make it? Most of us can point to a school or university chum with a fine future behind him or her. Top-of-the-class, seemingly having effortless brilliance, they ran away with all the prizes. Yet in terms of their working life, some really didn't fulfil their promise. In fact, some seem to have had astonishingly mediocre careers. Why is this?

There seem to be at least three reasons why this occurs. The *first* is because they can't, don't or won't accept *the rules*. They can't do "Corporate Man". They become known for their insubordination, disrespect for seniors (and procedures) and a taste for subversive anarchism.

Psychologists have a concept called "idiosyncratic credit," which refers to the fact that one has to obey the rules for a long time before being allowed to break them. People are allowed to be idiosyncratic once they have built up enough credit within the system.

Bright people can have a habit of asking good questions which upset those in power. As bright women have to learn faster than men, there is certainly a time when it pays to hide one's intelligence.

*Second*, bright people don't always make *good people decisions*. Psychological-mindedness and insight do not seem particularly related to cognitive ability. Choosing the wrong company, the wrong job or the wrong career path, can soon nullify the benefits of a big brain. Nearly all decisions involve more than pure hypothetico-deductive thinking. There are always ambiguities, uncertainties and unknowns. Wisdom is related to intelligence, but is only a part of it.

*Third*, and this is the point of the emotional intelligence lobby, some bright people fail because they are not very good at *social relationships*. You have to work with and through other people. You have to motivate and inspire them. Intelligence alone does not guarantee this. People can be too clever by half; too cognitive. They may be dismissive of those around them who are too slow to understand concepts. Good with ideas, bad with people.

# Spirituality at work

Work is often dedicated to material advancement and productivity. It is a social activity; while spirituality is often a personal endeavor. Work has mainly extrinsic rewards; spirituality mainly intrinsic ones. Spirituality at work is not just about business ethics and morality, however; it extends much further than that and has often been associated with a particular faith and religious condition. However, it is possible to have secular spirituality of the sort that people find in nature or even in poetry. The arts, particularly music, can have both short-term and enduring effects on the spiritual outlook of individuals.

The concept of spirituality at work has returned to capture the imagination of many in the West. It is clear that this is a very old concept and it remains a socio-historical question as to its demise and reappearance. Some argue that it is related to downsizing, globalization and greater job insecurity.

In Britain there was much surprise at the outpouring of public grief at the death of Diana, Princess of Wales. Social commentators, Church leaders and academics attempted to explain the acute and chronic grief reaction of so many. Britain was considered a post-Christian, postmodern, secular society famous for its scepticism and stoicism. Yet this event alerted people to the fact that there are powerful wells of spirituality in the nation that are apparently evident only at times of personal and national crisis.

A spiritual response can also be seen during times of economic crisis: when a company goes out of business or lays off staff. As well as anger there is often a remarkable spiritual change in the management and employees, frequently to their own surprise. Moreover increasing talk about the work–life balance is couched in the language of spirituality. The contrast is between the material and the spiritual; stress-inducer and stress-releaser; short-term and long-term; meaningless and meaningful work; less important and more important to the job-holder.

An increasing interest in workplace spirituality may be seen as a reaction to the demands of the modern work environment, where total commitment from individuals is required but without addressing some of the workers' fundamental needs.

More recently for social scientists, the concept of spirituality at work has surfaced in the concept of *spiritual intelligence*: the idea that spirituality is an ability as well as a preference. It is considered an individual difference factor that predicts how people behave in the workplace and elsewhere.

From the ability perspective, spiritual or existential intelligence is seen as a sensitivity to spiritual issues. The intriguing question, of course, is where that intelligence comes from – that is, its genetic/biological versus environmental determinants. Are people with more spiritual intelligence happier at work, more money conscious, and less stressed by work adversity?

Certainly there is a range of values that seems to fall under the umbrella of spirituality: accountability, compassion, cooperativeness, honesty, integrity, justice, respect, service and trustworthiness. Spirituality is a means, not an end. It encourages questions such as: Are our business decisions based exclusively on profit? Are employees required to sacrifice private/ family time to be successful? Are people becoming more self-centered and forgetting the principles of service to others in the wider community? Do employees get a sense of wonder at work? Do they have a sense of community?

Another theme rediscovered within the rubric of workplace spirituality is the concept of *vocation*: to work conscientiously and to celebrate all aspects of work's purpose. Indeed, the word "vocation" has always had both secular and spiritual significance: it can mean both a divine call to religious life as well as the work in which a person is regularly employed. It implies that the fit is right between person and organization, that they suit each other in terms of preferences, values and lifestyles.

Skeptics and cynics of the workplace spirituality concept are concerned by such things as the imposition of religious concepts or ethics of a particular religious group. Others are concerned by the superficiality and trivialization of religious and spiritual belief. Some are worried about cost, time-wasting and the potential harassment of the "non-spiritual." It has been suggested that the movement is in fact led by the baby-boomer generation who are now post-materialists and much more aware of their mortality. But it does seem to have "struck a nerve."

A focus on workplace spirituality makes the workplace somewhere to express and fulfill one's deeper purpose. More than 9 to 5; and "another day, another dollar." Work can and should be an integral part of one's life, and people do not disengage heart or brain at the factory door or office. People bring to work their attitudes, beliefs and values about both material and spiritual affairs. Even within more formal religious beliefs, historically there has not been a clear distinction between work and non-work. People do not suspend faith and values on entering the workplace. Personal ethics and values are relevant in nearly all aspects of work: from the very choice of vocation itself, to the treatment of colleagues and customers.

So, spirituality at work: sentimental, New Age nonsense, or a new and better conception of the modern workplace?

# Striving for power

There are many interesting but complicated theories of work motivation; partly because it is a fascinating and complex problem. We all know powerfully motivated people: the pathologically ambitious; the selfishly greedy; and the pathetic prize-seekers. They seem particularly goal-directed and obsessed about getting something, be it as intangible as respect and admiration or as concrete as their own private island or jet plane.

Psychologists have differed in the extent to which they believe people can access or accurately report on their real motives. The Freudians like to emphasize the unconscious nature of motives. In their opinion, there are dark forces, often repressed, and sometimes quite unacceptable (read sex and aggression) that are our real, hidden, motives. They are the cause of much of both misery and joy.

The social and cognitive psychologists, on the other hand, talk about life tasks, personal projects or strivings, current concerns or ultimate goals which human beings can, if they want to, report on accurately. In this sense we can know and articulate our motives.

David McClelland, arguably one of the greatest psychologists of the twentieth century, cut the Gordian knot of the motivational needs theorists, who had argued for years as to what fundamental motives were. According to McClelland, there were three, and only three: *the need for achievement, the need for affiliation* and *the need for power*.

The least studied – and perhaps the least interesting – is the need for affiliation. This is the motive to establish, maintain and restore friendship and friendly relations among family, acquaintances and work groups. We do so by friendly, nurturing and companionable activities and acts.

In contrast, the most studied is the need for achievement. McClelland saw this as the individual and group driver of economic success – the psychological equivalent of the work ethic.

The third motive is less talked about, but no less common or consequential: the need for power. Perhaps an unfortunate choice of term for the modern ear. Sounds a bit like Machiavellianism, manipulativeness and meddling. Desiring to be influential; wanting to have an impact.

Those with a strong power motive have an intense need for control and influence. They want to have an impact: on specific people, particular social groups and indeed the world at large. They achieve their ends by attempting to convince, influence and persuade others. Some try to influence by giving unsolicited help and advice; while others attempt to control or regulate others. The need for power is expressed by attempts to gain approbation and prestige, and have a perfect reputation.

In business, the need for achievement is more important for those who run their own businesses, but it is the reverse for those who manage businesses on behalf of others. Researchers have distinguished between good versus bad power needs, called the drive for socialized versus personalized power. It is about the use of power for institutionalized advancement over personal aggrandizement.

In an imaginative paper, the motivational researcher David Winter (2010) from the University of Michigan in the USA showed that achievement motivation predicted success in business but failure in politics.

Achievement motivation is associated with entrepreneurial success. Go to any MBA class for the evidence. Achievement motivation is associated with moderate risk-taking; assuming personal responsibility for results; using feedback to improve performance; and an expressive, restless style. It means goal-oriented, task-focused and energetic go-getters.

But the evidence suggests that this motive may not predict success in politics; indeed, almost the opposite. Perhaps that is why few successful business people make good politicians. Business people appointed to government often feel both disappointed and frustrated. And politicians, when they actually (on very rare occasions, fortunately) become business leaders, they are often abysmal failures.

Politicians worry about consistency, while business people are concerned with adaptation and change. Politicians have to compromise more than people in business. For politicians, the expenditure of energy ends with agreement, but for the business person it only begins with that; implementation is everything.

Business people like to have personal control over outcomes, but this is denied to politicians. So when things are difficult and important, the business leaders in politics resort to a range of tactics – micromanagement, bypassing legislators, using referendums, and dodgy, often illegal, acts – to gain control and make decisions.

Business and politics are different. Whereas politicians have to face and answer endless questions and criticism from many people, this is far less the case in business. The processes are more complex in politics; more people are involved. In business, there are a few very clear indicators of success and failure, usually to do with money.

Successful people score highly on both achievement and power motivation. Those with very high scores on achievement but average for power are seen as controlling and stable, demanding command and compliance using technical experts, and they can micromanage. Those scoring very highly on power but average on achievement thrive on negotiation and deal making, they talk about the "art of the possible" and are often charismatic, flamboyant and expressive.

So politicians may, out of necessity, be better team players. The boss is first among equals, not the fat controller. It's a complicated long game with moving force fields and multiple players. No wonder that the business executives who focus only on the bottom line don't do that well.

## Reference

Winter, D. (2010) "Why Achievement Motivation Predicts Success in Business but Failure in Politics," *Journal of Personality*, 78: 1637–68.

# Surveillance at work

Cameras in the street record our every move. Council officials go through our rubbish. Shops record all our purchases. The British are, it is said, the most spied on society of all time.

But it is the issue of electronic monitoring in the workplace that exercises people the most. Workplace surveillance has increased exponentially since the year 2000 and is likely to continue. Little cameras are everywhere; offices are "bugged" to detect heat or movement; and "smart chairs" can record how much they have been sat on every day.

There are essentially three reasons for this development. The *first* is related to spying and surveillance software. This has become smaller, cheaper and more powerful. The miniaturization of monitoring products means that they are now smaller and more easily hidden, thus becoming less controversial. And the average price per monitored employee has dropped dramatically. Your local corner shop now can afford to bristle with cameras.

The *second* is the opportunities of workers. Internet and email technologies have given even the lowliest of workers more options of how to spend their time. It is possible they have more opportunities than ever before to abuse and misuse their work time by doing all sorts of things on the internet. Well over two-thirds of people admit to going online regularly for personal reasons while they are at work. They book holidays, do internet shopping, play computer games and visit porn sites. Such fun, compared to the dreary business of spreadsheets. Indeed, disciplinary action, including dismissal, is now quite common for misuse of the internet.

*Third*, there have been changes in management styles, some believing that monitored employees are more focused and more productive than those who are less observed, or totally unmonitored. Surveillance concentrates the mind. Employers say that they monitor to improve *productivity* and around a third to reduce/prevent the *theft* of company property. Around a fifth claim that they monitor for *espionage* on the up- or downloading of confidential information to journalists, competitors or even tax authorities. A smaller number claim to use surveillance to prevent/reduce sexual and racial *harassment* or bullying.

There are many surveillance techniques. Telephones can be routinely tapped and all conversations recorded. Computer software offers such options as keystroke monitoring, screenshot capture, internet connections, email forwarding, content filtering and blocking, and remote freeze and lock-up.

Old-fashioned CCTV has become an art form. The observant or wary should try spotting the cameras in shops these days. And now there is the possibility of real-time surveillance. Through the use of GPS systems, all mobile phone owners can be followed wherever they go.

Some surveillance systems are *server-based* because they are network-wide, while others are *client-* or *host-based* because they are aimed at individual workers.

Perhaps the most interesting issue is the effect of surveillance on employees. What would you think or feel if you found out your employer was already doing some serious electronic monitoring of your workplace and equipment, or intended to do so in the future? Would it be worse if they were already doing it but had not told you? And would you believe all that old tosh about "for your protection" and "if you have nothing to hide…"?

There are some obvious issues that have been researched. Certainly, surveillance has a genuine potential to reduce trust, morale, creativity and support at work, all of which increase stress, alienation and, para-doxically, secrecy. But the real question is cause and effect. Do employers introduce surveillance because there is a lack of trust, or vice versa? And with ambulance-chasing lawyers increasingly interested in the workplace, it is no wonder that there has been an increase in surveillance litigation, with electronically monitored employees filing privacy lawsuits against their employers.

The law of unintended consequences appears to be at work. Cameras increase stress and anxiety and reduce productivity. Workers are fright-ened to take breaks and have an increased risk of repetitive strain injuries. One case occurred where a boss constantly flashed a message to a lowly (easily and heavily monitored) data processor: "You are working less hard than the person next to you." This increased anxiety and as a result low-ered productivity.

Equally interesting, the technology designed to improve communica-tion reduces it. People chat less, help each other less and say less.

There are, of course, ethical and legal issues and hazards for employ-ers interested in introducing new, cheap technology aimed at spying on their employees. And there can be some tempting dilemmas associated with the electronic monitoring of hackers and terrorists. The issues are: what is being monitored, how is it done, and why?

Surveillance infringes privacy, period. It can break, or make it harder to establish, trusting relationships. It gives power to Big Brother and turns workplaces into total institutions, like prisons. But worse, it can increase the problem that it was introduced to counteract. It can start a vicious cycle of organizational deviance. The reason is usually because surveillance attacks the symptoms of problems rather than their causes.

The more control and the more autonomy people have at work are good direct indices of their satisfaction and stress levels. Surveillance need not necessarily interfere with these. But just that feeling of being constantly snooped on does change the feel of a place.

# Taking care and taking charge

Want to take part in a fun study? See below the list below of typical, relevant, leadership behaviors:

1. *Consulting*: checking with others before making decisions and plans.
2. *Delegating*: authorizing others to have substantial responsibility.
3. *Influencing upward*: appealing to those at the top.
4. *Inspiring*: motivating others to greater commitment and enthusiasm.
5. *Mentoring*: facilitating skill development and career advancement.
6. *Networking*: developing and maintaining useful relationships.
7. *Problem solving*: analyzing, identifying and acting decisively to remove work impediments.
8. *Rewarding*: providing recognition, praise and remuneration for good work.
9. *Supporting*: assisting and encouraging others, and allocating resources to help.
10. *Team building*: encouraging cooperation and constructive conflict resolution.

Now think of some senior managers in your organization. Thinking of the men first, what percentage of them demonstrate each of the leadership behaviors listed to a significant degree? And then do the same for the female managers – in the hope that you have enough of them to make a reasonable judgment.

This is what two consultants and an American academic asked nearly 30 senior managers to do (see Prime *et al.* 2009). Male managers are seen to do problem solving, delegating and influencing upward well. And the women are good at supporting, team building and rewarding.

The paper is called "Women Take Care, Men Take Charge." It's a title echoing John Gray's book, *Men Are from Mars, Women Are from Venus*. It concerns the widespread belief that the average woman possesses fewer leadership traits than the typical man, and tends to be much less task-oriented. Women do the soft stuff: the morale building; the social support function, but men bite the bullet: set directions; get the show on the road. Men, it is argued, are "naturally endowed" with those special prerequisite qualities for leadership ... and women aren't.

It is a courageous or stupid male who dares to wander into this territory. The vulgar evolutionary theorist will be shot down by a growing hunt of social theorists crying "nurture not nature!" The whole idea of sex differences seems to have strong pendulum swings. With the grow of feminism in the 1980s researchers were eager to show either that there were essentially no significant inherited differences between men and women, or else that the differences one saw could and should be attributed mainly to socialization. It was a battle between sex and gender; and it is one unlikely to end.

However, in recent years there have been many careful scholarly works that have picked over the evidence cautiously and critically. And, of course, the conclusion is that things are somewhat more complicated than was originally thought, with a good deal of interaction between genes and the environment. But hard science does not interest policy-makers or pressure groups; unless, of course, the science is seen to support their position uncritically.

The question that exercises the academics is threefold. *First*, is there any evidence that these gender-at-work stereotypes carry a grain of truth? *Second*, if these are stereotypes, what are the consequences for promotion and pay for women in organizations? And, *third*, what should we do about the situation?

Despite the fact that there are far fewer female than male managers, studies have been done on sex differences in leadership styles. It was difficult research: finding males and females in equivalent jobs, sectors, areas and levels so that one can attribute any differences that are observed to sex/gender effects rather than some other factor such as age, education, intelligence or personality variables. The answer came back: there are more similarities than differences; and gender is not a reliable indicator of the way that a particular person leads. There may be difficult styles, but successful leaders all have to do essentially the same things: get together, motivate and direct teams to achieve stretching goals.

So, the theory is more a stereotype than a reality. What data we have on this topic suggests fewer differences than one might expect.

What are the consequences of the stereotype? Fewer women at the top; and those that are, are paid less. Worse, they appear to be evaluated less favorably, possibly because people apply lower standards when evaluating men. And successful female leaders are judged to be more hostile. Some have suggested that they are also appointed to high office only when there are serious problems and they are likely to fail. This, of course, confirms the idea that they are not really competent in the first place.

So, what is to be done, if anything? Perhaps reduce the "unfair" stereotype-based evaluations used in appraisals of women. Get more behavioral and specific: what does problem-solving competency look like? This demonstrably reduces all sorts of bias. Develop "weighting criteria" (for example, the way in which women and men are scored) to try to ensure that both men and women are judged by the same standards. Have, as the Scandinavians do, quotas of women for senior positions.

But everything must rest on the quality and quantity of the evidence for actual sex differences in leadership style *and* effectiveness. Is it clear or unequivocal there are no real differences? And if so, why do gender stereotypes arise and linger? Thus, the favorite academic conclusion ... more research needs to be done.

## Reference

Prime, J., Carter, N. and Welbourne, T. (2009) "Women 'Take Care'; Men 'Take Charge'," *Psychologist-Manager Journal*, 12; 25–49.

# Taking offense

The quite disproportionate influence of negative over positive information is well known. One error, one misjudgment, one infelicitous remark and one can be branded with the mark of Cain.

People often justly complain that their successes are never remembered yet their failures are never forgotten. One off-guard aside and the forces of darkness arrive to punish you. Recall Carol Thatcher's "gollywog" remark in a TV studio, and her swift punishment. Or Lord Young, who dared to imply that times weren't that bad at all, with interest rates being so low.

Someone, somewhere took umbrage. The remark was something "ist:" racist, sexist, fattist or, if you can't think of something specific enough, then fascist. A current popular trigger word is "homophobic", though phobia implies fear rather than anything else. At any rate, a remark can be seen as deeply offensive to ... and here you can list groups from the disabled to migrants.

People at work seem to be no exception to the "negative trumps positive" rule. And a lot of people know this and use it to their own advantage. They are quick to take offense; to be affronted; to have righteous indignation. They seem easily insulted. And hence the respect agenda.

Are some people more easily offended than others? Certainly. But why? Are they more fragile, more insecure or simply nastier? Have they not heard that sticks and stones may break your bones but words will never hurt you?

Should sensitivity to offense become a new mental illness like adult defiant disorder? Or is it so common now that it is considered to be quite normal? Like the condition known as passive-aggressive personality disorder, which was dropped from the nomenclature because it was so widespread.

Perhaps it's like bullying: there is evidence that bullies and the bullied share similar characteristics. They are lower than average on social skills; less assertive, less persuasive and less charming. Perhaps those who give and take offense readily also share certain characteristics. They are not too hot in sending or interpreting signals. They read too little or too much into the conversation.

The question is what to do if someone takes offense. Of course, the offense may have been meant: the punch well landed. But what if a chance remark or behavior results in an angry display of disgust? The question is, what to do? One school says quite simply, never say sorry, never apologize. It only encourages them. If meant, they deserved it. If not, there is nothing to apologize for.

While theologians have always studied apologetics – the reasoned defence of a belief system – there is a new subdiscipline called *customer apologetics*. This involves the question of how and when to respond to customer complaints. There are a number of options here: ignore them; begin a series of increasingly grovelling "mea culpa" letters; offer some petty token; offer a more serious token; or cough up.

It's called "business recovery," and hotels, airlines and restaurants allocate big resources to it. The paradox is this: if you upset a customer through a mistake and you quickly fix it, they are happier than if you hadn't made the mistake in the first place. And because repeat, loyal customers are so essential to those sectors, keeping them is pretty important. A loyal broadcaster of your virtues can so easily turn into a consumer terrorist happy to see you really suffer.

But what of the personal apology? We have seen a lot of this recently. Poor old Boris Johnson, the Mayor of London, traipsing up to Liverpool when he was editor of the *Spectator* magazine to be humiliated on local radio because of a chance remark. And the many times the sacked Peter Mandelson had to apologize for his mistakes, which now seem to be happily forgotten.

For students of beneficial apologia for insults, there are three things that have to be done. *First*, sincerely express regret about what you did. Do it simply and clearly. *Second*, admit that it was a poor example of mature, adult, responsible behavior. And *third*, assure people that it won't happen again.

It might have been a personal failure of taste and judgment, not aiming to offend but obviously succeeding in doing so. Best not go for a complex explanation of why you said what you did, based on some obscure lexical, historical or personal custom. And best not to try some defence such as that you were tired and emotional, heavy with a cold, or unaware you were being recorded. And don't attack those who have been offended under any circumstances. That would only serve to compound the problem.

Yet offense-taking seems to have reached epidemic proportions. All rather too similar to the "compensation culture" that has been imported into Britain from America. There are codes for insults. One begins by saying "With all due respect..." (and always means the exact opposite).

One's opponents may be "learned friends" or even "most honorable." There are memorable phrases to use. You are not a liar: you are "economical with the truth." Your ideas are not poorly thought through, just "somewhat premature." One learns to say "If you say so…," meaning "That's complete rubbish."

It's called etiquette and euphemism. It's an art form and huge fun. It's the British middle-class articulate way of being insulting, demeaning and hypercritical of people without resorting to a direct insult. That is the most prized skill: never to give offense but to be pretty frank in one's opinion.

# To do a Ph.D.

The further the halcyon days of undergraduate life recede, the happier and more content they appear to have been. Wistful memories of days spent in a punt; brilliant lectures by erudite dons; passionate debates fueled by cheap red wine; and, most delightfully, sex in the afternoon. And universities are eager to cash in on those happy memories in their donation-oriented, ever glossier magazines.

So perhaps not surprisingly, one manifestation of a midlife crisis, is to "think about" doing a Ph.D. People might be stuck in a rut (at any age), or feel they need a change. "Empty nesters," those who have "achieved financial independence," some wanting a career switch – all types consider the idea.

They have numerous fantasies about the Ph.D. All that "free time" to develop potentially brilliant ideas. The company of all those other seriously bright people. The book(s) that might result. And, of course, being called Doctor. Memories of those glorious summers and fantasies about a sublime, stress-free, book-lined future seem irresistible.

But what about the reality? Few people have come into contact with a Ph.D. Most have not talked to those who are "writing up". And clearly none have spoken to those many part-timers, as well as full-timers, who dropped out.

There are a number of factors that should make the idealist cautious. First, the cost. At the time of writing, a Ph.D. would cost an adult around £100,000, possibly more. Where does this figure come from? On average, a Ph.D. takes three to four years to complete. Assuming an opportunity cost based on the average wage, this will be around £60,000. Most potential Ph.D. students should be earning more, so this is a pretty conservative amount. Add to this the fees, living costs and sundries at, let's say, £15,000 a year, and we get another £50,000.

So it's a six-figure number for a piece of paper that guarantees nothing. It might be a great experience, but then it should be for that amount of money.

Next, a Ph.D. is essentially an apprenticeship in skills. Just as in the medieval guilds, when one "learned the trade" by being apprentice to a master. Indeed, the concept of master classes has recently been revived. Lawyers and accountants still go through a similar process. It can be slow and tedious, and is certainly expensive, but it is considered the best way to do things. Ph.D. students learn the skills of their trade: doing good, publishable research in a particular speciality.

Everything, however, depends on the supervisor(s) ... not on the reputation of the university or the department, but the skill, temperament, ability and above all motivation of the supervisor, who has many roles to play. They are "in loco parentis," but are also teacher and exemplar; instructor and model; educator and counsellor.

It is a difficult and complex relationship. Both student and teacher may have different needs and styles, which can make the relationship fraught. The anxious, dependent student and the cavalier supervisor; and the brilliant but lazy student and the conscientious supervisor could both lead to difficulties. Personalities, values and ability differences can cause unforeseen and tricky problems. And, at least in the sciences, Ph.D. work may be team-work. The brilliant don has a large team; the lab has a program and you are expected to slot into it.

Students have to acquire the skills of the discipline. They have to learn how to access and evaluate current learning. They have to learn technical skills as well as advanced numeracy and literacy. They need to acquire presentation skills. And perhaps, more important, how to handle biting, sometimes anonymous, criticism ... and rejection.

Some students arrive with many of the necessary skills pretty advanced. Indeed, by the end of the Ph.D., it is not unusual for the student to be more skilled than the supervisor, particularly when it comes to technical issues. Inevitably, the techies are not so hot on writing, while the scribblers can't always easily pick up the technology.

A British Ph.D. is examined orally. Having read the thesis in detail, two examiners grill the candidate for anything between two and six hours. Very few pass outright. They may have to make minor or major alterations, the latter taking as much as another year of work. Less happy outcomes include a downgrade to a master's degree or a downright failure.

Examiners look for many things: command and critical reading of the current literature; a mastery of the methodology in pertinent areas; the ability to formulate and answer good questions/hypotheses; and whether parts of the thesis are publishable according to the peer-review criteria.

Originality and innovation are, curiously, not the paramount criteria. Naïve applicants have the image of Ph.D. research being characterized by startling originality. And so it may be. Indeed it's good if this occurs, but it must also be accompanied by evidence of technical skill.

The Worshipful Company of Doctors of Philosophy, as with all guilds, strives to keep up standards; to admit only those whose apprenticeship has fulfilled the exacting criteria of the day.

Three to five years of intellectual stimulation, self-fulfillment and the opportunity to be creative and discover your talents. Or a hard slog, in abject poverty, with few opportunities to recover your financial investment.

# What is conscientiousness?

How relevant is the work ethic today? The answer: very, and as much as always. Yet the concept of the (Protestant) work ethic brings with it a significant amount of theological and socio-political baggage.

It goes back over 100 years, when two German writers, Max Weber and Karl Marx, challenged each other. Weber's thesis was that it is religious beliefs and practices, not economic forces, that create wealth. The hard-working, ascetic and rational Protestants of the time invested their money wisely, admired entrepreneurial spirit and grew wealthy. They saw economic success as a sign of God's grace, but they were encouraged not to spend their money on frivolities and pleasure but to invest it wisely. This also led, some argued, to the distinction between the undeserving poor (those who are lazy, feckless and idle) and the deserving poor, whose circumstances were beyond their control. This thesis has been picked over by economists, historians and theologians ever since.

Psychologists were late entrants to the debate. They thought it was "achievement motivation" that was the driver. The personal need to get on, get ahead, make one's mark. It was considered to be a deep-seated drive; a need that had to be fulfilled through personal success. And this drive was believed to have originated from very particular parenting. Parents who set high standards and used firm discipline, who believed in and modelled the postponement of gratification, who stressed independence and rationality, and encouraged the work ethic in their children. The work ethic is not inherited genetically, but it may be hard to socialize this into adults if they have not acquired its basic principles as children.

Recently, however, the personality psychologists have identified the work ethic and need-for-achievement beliefs and behaviors as a *personality trait*; something that is stable over time and explains a great deal of social and work-related behavior. And it is one of the most important characteristics for employers to search out in candidates for employment.

After intelligence, the best predictor of school, university and work success is conscientiousness. This accounts for why girls do better at school than boys. It predicts when and why people pitch up and pitch in. Conscientious people have a very low incidence of absences and disciplinary problems. They also tend to do well, though the trait is not particularly related to leadership. That takes a rather different sort of (political) skill. Conscientiousness is singularly and particularly "desirable."

So, two relevant questions: Precisely what is conscientiousness – what are the components or facets? And equally important, how do you measure it?

The taxonomists of conscientiousness argue that there are eight distinguishable but related parts:

1. *Industriousness*: this is about working hard, always putting in an effort and frequently exceeding expectations. Industrious people push themselves (and others) very hard to succeed.
2. *Perfectionism*: this is aiming for high quality, no mistakes, no rejected work. It is about detail orientation and striving always to be the best.
3. *Tidiness:* this is a strong preference for order, regularity and the philosophy of "everything-in-its-place." Conscientious people have a strong aversion to disorder and mess. They like things correctly filed and tasks completed.
4. *Avoidance of procrastination*: those who are really conscientious are not the type to be distracted easily, or have difficulty in getting started. They don't put off all unpleasant tasks, and start on only the easy ones. They get to work at once, prioritizing and spending their time and effort wisely.
5. *A preference for control*: this should not be confused with "control freakery." It's about planning, being thoughtful and decisive. It is also about understanding the role of authority. The opposite is rushed, rash and impulsive behavior.
6. *Caution*: because of the above traits, the conscientious individuals are careful to avoid mistakes, to get their facts right and to think ahead. They think before they speak, choosing their words carefully.
7. *Task planning*: conscientious individuals are organized. They carefully devise a plan, a schedule, a considered path, then they stick to it and require others to do likewise. They like to work out efficient routines and stick to them.
8. *Perseverance*: conscientious people deal well with frustrations and setbacks. They don't give up easily, don't try to avoid responsibility, and don't lose interest. They are calm under pressure.

It's better to work for a conscientious boss. They roll up their sleeves and pitch in. They take responsibility for their actions ... and more relevantly, they have a social conscience – that still, quiet voice that tells them not to let themselves and others down.

The second question posed above was how to measure conscientious-ness in individuals. There are plenty of questionnaires available, but they are prone to impression management and self-delusional bias. It's prob-ably best to ask others – teachers, managers, work subordinates – who know the individual. It's not difficult to see the listed behaviors and their consequences. Teachers, lecturers and supervisors are accurate informers of the above characteristics, or lack of them.

But could someone become too conscientious? Is the over-tidy per-fectionist perhaps suffering from a mild form of OCD? As with all other traits, one can have too much of a good thing.

# Whistle-blowing at work

Whistle-blowers: courageous, moral heroes who expose organizational wrongdoing; or angry, vengeful and often second-rate employees trying to get their own back? Should organizations encourage or discourage whistle-blowing? Will it be a healthy, moral safety valve or an encouragement to disaffected, alienated and vindictive employees to attempt to get revenge?

From the company perspective, the whistle-blower is often seen as disloyal, a traitor, one who indulges in tittle-tattle, but from the bottom-up perspective they can be seen as heroes: courageous fighters for truth. Whistle-blowers talk of personal sacrifice for a noble cause; acting because they had no choice; and being unable not to act, knowing what they knew. There is much talk about identification with victims, a sense of collective guilt and shame (working for the company), even being a part of history.

Whistle-blowing is often a serious act. "Just" whistle-blowers need to be completely sure of their facts and have sufficient reliable and robust evidence to stand up in a court of law.

But it is quite simply too easy to be a whistle-blower: media experts tell of how frequently they are called by people with all sorts of impossible stories and little evidence to support them. Their motives are often a curious mix of the personal and the political. Justice, ethics and fairness are concepts that are bandied about. But the motives behind them may be quite different.

When are whistle-blowers effective? Most, it seems, go public once organizations attempt to cover up wrongdoing and retaliate against the whistle-blower. Where whistle-blowers are powerful, with unique skills, resources and secrets that the organization needs (and cannot easily replace), they are more likely to succeed. The more competent, confident, credible and objective they seem to be, the more they are listened to. Experts with legitimate power are likely to be more effective, particularly with internal whistle-blowing.

There are three "actors" in every whistle-blowing case: *the wrongdoer(s)*, the *whistle-blower* and the *recipient of the information*. From a legal perspective, whistle-blowing is warranted if the person *believes in good faith* that the wrongdoing has implications for policy. From a philosophical perspective, the question arises as to whether the act is ethical. But, of course, there are different and mutually antagonistic ethical positions. One man's meat ... and all that.

Whistle-blowers need to decide whether to use internal or external channels for complaint. They are clearly very different in outcome. Whistle-blowers need a reasonable supposition of success in that they believe their actions will lead to the wrongdoing being stopped, as opposed to receiving sanctions against themselves.

So when is whistle-blowing justified? This refers to the *manner* as well as the *reasons* for it. Those who believe whistle-blowing to be a good thing talk of the suppression of dissent and give advice on how to be an effective resister. Whistle-blowing has been portrayed as an effective anti-corruption device.

Some organizations, clearly worried by the threat of whistle-blowing – often referred to more euphemistically as "raising concerns at work" – have policies and procedures to deal with it. Thus they may have an employee called the "whistle-blowing champion" and set out whom to contact, how "the investigation" is dealt with by internal inquiry, and what occurs if the whistle-blower is still not satisfied. The process is detailed on the organization's website, almost as a badge of pride – a sort of "investors in morality."

It is, however, sensible to put into practice *whistle-blowing procedures* stating that the issue of malpractice is taken seriously and will be dealt with firmly. Employees must have the right to raise issues confidentially and without fear of repercussions. There must also be guidelines and time-limits for the consequent investigations. Importantly, all the procedures should specify consequences and penalties for making false and malicious allegations.

How can organizations prevent or deal with corruption and wrong-doing before whistle-blowers feel the need to report on what they see and hear? The following are options:

- *Whistle-blower hotlines*, which allow employees to make anonymous complaints to trained staff. Do they work? The jury is still out on this. Some believe that they backfire, encouraging petty complaints by disgruntled staff and can make the organization look bad in the eyes of the public. What difference does it make if potential whistle-blowers are not allowed anonymity, if the process is outsourced? Some argue the signal-to-noise ratio is so bad that there are 10 trivial, minor, unsubstantiated complaints for every real one.

- *Ethical training*, which may include workshops that employees attend at induction, promotion and so on, and that help employees to discuss and think about how they should respond if they are confronted by wrongdoing.
- Having a clear, open and efficient *investigative process* known to all so that whistle-blowers can anticipate and trust exactly what is going to happen.
- Having good *management processes* in the first place that are fair and robust, and not precisely the opposite of what they say they are. All employees are sensitive to hypocrisy. Indeed, it may well be that blundering cover-up tactics by managers to reduce whistle-blowing actually encourages it.

Ambulance-chasing lawyers and the American litigious culture means that whistle-blowing is a big issue. But now whistle-blowers go straight to the internet and social websites to spread their "news," thus making all those carefully-thought-out plans worth very little.

# Wit at work

Funny ha ha, funny pathetic, funny peculiar. How often are people landed in hot water through their supposed sense of humor? Of the many unpleasant things we have inherited from America, one is humorless, litigious, killjoy behavioral requirements. "It was meant as a joke" doesn't sound too good in the courtroom or the cold in-house inquiry room. How many have been punished for an offhand *double entendre*?

What is the function of humor? Which types of humor are acceptable and which forbidden? What are the consequences of stamping on those who use verbal wit?

Why do some people enjoy aggressive or sexual humor, while others prefer the intellectual or black types? Is personality related to humor creation; for example, telling jokes, making puns? Do people who can make us laugh have quite different personality traits from those who do not or cannot?

Are professional humorists clearly distinguishable as creators versus performers of humor, and do both differ in personality terms from amateur humorists? Some researchers have been particularly interested in the social function of humor. The fascination is in how humor can generate a sense of group solidarity/belongingness, provide a safety valve for dealing with group pressure, and help individuals to cope with threatening, negative experiences.

The ancient Greeks saw humor as being related to "the humors" and, clearly, sanguine types were more humorous than melancholic types. But humor creation seems unrelated to humor appreciation. The former is concerned with perceiving and describing people, objects or situations in an incongruous way (that is, humorously), while the latter is the enjoyment of these descriptions.

Thus we have four possible types: namely individuals who are high/high (frequently making witty remarks/jokes and seeking out other people or situations where there is humor); low/low (serious people who do not enjoy telling or hearing humorous stories); high/low (people who enjoy telling jokes but show little appreciation when told them by others); and low/high (people who are not much given to creating humor, but who love to laugh and do so frequently). There clearly are different types of humor: nonsense humor based on puns or incongruous combinations of words or images; satire based on ridiculing people, groups or institutions; aggressive humor that describes brutality, violence, insults and sadism; and sexual humor. And, of course, the British speciality: scatological, or toilet humor.

Sigmund Freud wrote a number of papers on humor, and was clearly fascinated by its functions, as well as by the techniques/mechanics of making jokes. Jokes, like dreams, provide an insight into the unconscious. They are important defence mechanisms, and suppressing them can lead to serious consequences. Freud divided jokes into two classes, namely the innocent/trivial and the tendentious. The latter served two major purposes – aggression (satire) or sex. Thus the purpose of the most interesting jokes is the expression of sexual or aggressive feelings that would otherwise be barred. Furthermore, the amount and timing of laughter correspond to the psychical energy saved by not having to repress: "In jokes veritas: jokes are a socially accepted and socially shared mechanism of expressing what is normally forbidden."

Freudian theory is a fecund source of testable hypotheses. For example, individuals who find aggressive jokes the funniest will be those in whom aggression is normally repressed. Those whose main defence mechanism is repression and who have a strong social conscience will be humorless (they will not laugh at jokes); wits will be more neurotic than the normal population; and highly repressed individuals prefer jokes with complex mechanisms over "simple" jokes.

But what of humor preference? Extraverts tend to like fast jokes (skits/comedy) and practical jokes. They can take jokes at their own expense and approve of others who can laugh at themselves. Some neurotic and unstable people like satire and black humor, but tend not to enjoy humor much. Worse, they fail to appreciate the possible uses of humor as an antidote to their anxiety, moodiness and depression. Equally, they fail to appreciate others who use humor as a coping mechanism – as a way to attack and distort reality and thus make things more tolerable.

Many professional humorists are notably introverted – serious people who are not much prone to laughter. Writers are more introverted than performers, but even the latter tend to be unstable (neurotic), and characterized by anxiety, depression and low self-esteem. However, they find that their humor gives them power over others and an ability to compensate for their feelings of inferiority.

The problem with humor at work is that it is very subjective. And the humorless will inherit the earth because they have been rewarded for "telling nanny." There are, of course, occasions when "humor" is totally inappropriate and insulting, but often jokes, like hearing aids, are in the ear of the beholder.

Humor at work is bound up with corporate culture: racism lingering just below the surface can been seen in some jokes. But be very careful about any sexist or sexual joke in any quasi- or crypto-egalitarian or puritan organization. That can be totally career limiting. And as for public schoolboy practical jokers ... there are now armies of lawyers who have given up ambulance chasing for the more lucrative mobile-phone recordings of the odd joke in the work place.

# The work ethic

So Niall Ferguson (perhaps currently the world's most famous historian) agrees with Max Weber? The work ethic will save us and make us rich. It is the philosophical and moral glue that made us masters of the universe.

Weber was a polymath, whose training in economics, law and sociology enabled him to understand the complexity of organizations. He is well known for his research on two topics: the Protestant work ethic (PWE) and bureaucracy.

His argument was that Protestantism was associated with wealth and success as a result of various beliefs: that all work is good and ultimately for God's glory (the doctrine of calling); the signs of God's grace can be seen in this world and its monetary success (doctrine of predestination); wealth is to be amassed and invested but not spent (doctrine of asceticism); and we are all responsible for our own actions and must be rational in decision-making (doctrine of sanctification).

The PWE places a universal taboo on *idleness*, and *industriousness* is considered a religious ideal; *waste* is a vice, and *frugality* a virtue; *complacency* and *failure* are outlawed and sinful, and *ambition* and *success* are taken as sure signs of God's favor; the universal sign of sin is *poverty*, and the crowning sign of God's favor is *wealth*.

The broader meaning of the PWE typically refers to one or more of the following beliefs:

- People have a religious obligation to fill their lives with hard work, effort and even drudgery, which are to be valued for their own sake; physical pleasures and enjoyments are to be shunned; and an ascetic existence of disciplined routine and rigor is the only acceptable way to live.
- Men and women are expected to spend long hours at work, with little or no time for personal recreation and leisure, which only lead to vice. A worker should have a dependable attendance record, with low absenteeism and tardiness.
- Workers should be highly productive, and produce a large quantity of goods or provide a service for everyone's sake as well as to take pride in their work and do their jobs well.
- Employees should have feelings of (total) commitment and loyalty to their profession, their company and their work group.

- Workers should be achievement-oriented and should constantly strive for promotion and advancement. High-status jobs with prestige and the respect of others are important indicators of a "good" person.
- People should acquire wealth through honest labor and retain it through thrift and wise investments. Frugality is desirable; extravagance and waste should be avoided.

At the centre of the concept of the PWE are values and beliefs such as taking personal responsibility for actions, the postponement of gratification, and asceticism, which actually lead to economic success on both an individual and a national level.

It is an ideology for today: the spirit of enterprise. It still makes sense. Because pessimistic Calvinists were so concerned with scarcity, they stressed the need for *productive work* to bring about *surpluses*. They encouraged the propensity to save – the maximization of productivity and *minimization of consumption* were ethically important, and saving seemed a most useful solution. Saving was more acceptable than spending, and investing more acceptable than saving, because charging interest was taboo.

The PWE is associated *with accounting* – effective efficiency means knowledge of, and ability in, making calculations of input and output, demand and supply, cost, price and profits. Quantitative skills became professionalized – profit-making as a calling, with profit maximization being the prime objective. The *acquisition instinct* became a Utopian idea. Anything that increases net profit is good and anything that lowers it is bad. Labor *per se* is only good when it becomes efficient, cost-reducing and effective.

Marketing helped the purchaser to consume more effectively, and hence the producer to produce more efficiently. The ad-men are OK. The promotion of products through advertising was given ethical support because self- and other material improvement was considered to be morally desirable.

The new "would-be saints" were successful entrepreneurs, captains of industry, elected political leaders, certified men of knowledge and accepted opinion leaders. All organizations were turned into meritocratic *democracies*. Liberty and equality were promoted, as was mobility, a democratized social structure and so on.

The PWE philosophy was individualistic and *against government interference*, nonconformist and against conflict and militant behavior.

It tended to retreat from conflict and be anti-authoritarian. PWE endorsers were upward-moving, middle-class-oriented and tried to resolve conflicting claims of meritocratic elitism and egalitarianism.

Weber's thesis has been under attack for over 100 years. Some argued that his understanding of Protestant theology was erroneous. Similarly, he misunderstood Catholic doctrine, particularly as it differed on economic detail. The data Weber used to support his thesis were limited mainly to Anglo-Saxon material, while other European data fail to support his hypothesis. Weber's distinction between modern and earlier forms of capitalism was unwarranted, because the spirit of "modern" capitalism was apparent in earlier periods. The supposed causal correlation between Puritanism and modern capitalism is unfounded. Blah, blah, blah....

In spite of historical "ifs-and-buts," the PWE was clearly a major force in shaping the modern economy. But do we still believe in it? Do young people adhere to it? Will it be enough to get the West out of the crisis that began in 2007? We'll see....

# Writing as therapy

Psychotherapy is often called the "talking cure." Whether you are an Adlerian, Freudian, Jungian, or even unfashionably Kleinian, most of the cure involves natter. Well, that's not strictly the case: it's really a monologue. Sometimes these therapy sessions are called "expensive conversations."

Others have climbed on the ladder. Indeed, there is a cornucopia of therapeutic options mainly, but not exclusively, involving talk. So there is Rogerian nondirective counselling, and Reichian screaming. You can talk alone or in groups; you can burble and blub; but "getting it out" is seen as the key.

And there is now an expanding business version of the above: coaching and mentoring. Needless to say, these share many business values, predominant among them being time and money. Coaching costs a lot but takes relatively short periods of time, sceptics might point out. The line between being a confessor, a confidant, a coach or a counsellor is not that clear, as they are all in much the same business.

Some sceptics have lamented the decline of the stoical, stiff-upper-lip sangfroid of the British. They point to a wave of therapism where the mildest life setback seems to call for a trauma counsellor, a relationship therapist or a self-esteem educator. What happened to that uncomplaining "we can take it" spirit of the Blitz ... or was that just clever propaganda?

So we now have a curious array of people happy to call themselves an "emotion ventilationist," a "traumatologist," or a "recoverist," and who, of course, want everyone to be in therapy for everything. And despite their so-called disapproval of labelling, are happy to describe their opponents as "denialists," thus subtly echoing the climate and holocaust sceptics.

This is the old argument between "sensitizers" and "repressors." The former see "letting it all hang out" as an element essential to well-being; while the latter think that "putting it out of the mind and keeping busy" is much more beneficial. The latter argue that the former leads to self-indulgence, self-pity and addiction to introspection, while the former see the stoical repressors as being emotionally buttoned-up and out of touch with their emotions.

And the research literature is, as ever, rather equivocal about which approach is better. It's a case of horses for courses: it depends on the person, the problem, the therapist and the therapy.

But there is another type of therapy that has been known to many over the years: writing. Poets, for example, have encapsulated great pain and pleasure as well as awe and wonderment in spare and beautifully crafted words.

In recent decades there has been a resurgence in the therapeutic power of writing. Old people are encouraged to write down their memories. Prisoners too are encouraged first to learn to write and then to tell their story.

The question is, in what sense is writing therapeutic? It clearly involves some serious introspection: an attempt to make sense of the past, and to examine it from various angles rather than simply trying to shift blame on to others.

This is much more than trying to write pretty sentences. It is about singling out experiences, events and people that have contributed to one's life. Seeing cause and effect, understanding psychological processes, can significantly increase self-understanding. Suddenly things become apparent: patterns are observed, and explanations become obvious.

Writing is often redemptive. And it helps because it nearly always involves some commitment to change. Autobiographical writing is about the past – "another country". A place where things were done differently. A place of no return. Hence the journey theme in so many accounts. So now one can move on: can change.

In counselling they call this the "therapeutic alliance." It's the feeling that one is better accepted, respected and understood by the therapist "to whom all hearts are open, all desires known." The same is true of the reaction of readers. Old people, prisoners, disturbed children and so on are often surprised and delighted by the reaction of others to their stories. People take an interest and many writers feel they become allies, helping each other in the journey.

One consequence of writing one's story leads to an interest in the experiences of others. It stimulates the reading of other autobiographies, particularly of those who have had similar experiences.

And there is now a veritable cornucopia of writings to choose from. Alas, perhaps, the "confessional" autobiography has become very popular. There are now dozens of agonizing books about child abuse by parents, priests and relatives. One suspects the popularity of this genre is, in some cases, a motive for writing the book and exaggerating the issues.

Of course, writing a book is not necessarily confined only to the literate. Dictation and transcription are possible. Indeed, many writers do dictate, pacing up and down and hearing as much as tasting their own words.

It does take some effort. Most people begin with classes. The "writer in residence," the eclectic therapist, the insightful carer often have to persuade the doubting and diffident person in their care to have a go. We hear, of course, nearly always, only the success stories, and clearly, writing does not work for all.

But it is amazingly cheap and effective. And possibly also non-addictive. Scribble yourself well. Sack your coach and buy a laptop.

# Writing your own obituary

A surprisingly large number of people start their day by reading the obituary column of their preferred newspaper. Some, the old saying goes, do it to establish that they are still alive. Obituaries are a wonderful way to mark the passage of time; to look back, and to evaluate not only a life but also an era. They are indeed historical records: a window into an age and a catalogue of deeds of important people.

There are, of course, professional newspaper, radio and television obituary writers and producers. For the very famous and the very old their obits are "on the blocks" or "in the can" often years before they actually die. Individuals, aware of this, have asked to read or view their own obits … not always with total approval.

It is said that Alfred Nobel, he of the Prize, read his own obit which had been printed in error, and was horrified at what he read. It said "the merchant of death is dead." That shook him up so much that he promptly gave all his money away to found those most cherished of prizes. And, of course, Charles Dickens' *Christmas Carol* was a parable of redemption after considering the life one has led.

It is not only the great and the good (old soldiers, scientists, statesmen) who appear in these columns, but also maverick individuals who have attracted sufficient attention in their lifetimes. "Characters," oddballs, life-enhancers, people from "another time" make it into the obituaries pages. Pretenders in both senses of the word: obscure Mitteleuropean royalty; con-artists and charlatans; alcoholic, self-destructive minor authors; practically certifiable clergymen and so on. It is a sign of great distinction, though, alas, one can never be sure of what will be written about one or, worse, whether anything will be written about one all.

Obits are such a source of interest and consternation that they provoke letters to the editor, rejoinders, addenda. Most relate little anecdotes that illustrate the very essence of the deceased. Some, but very few, take issue with the obituary writers by saying the late lamented was a "devious devil," a "selfish shyster," or an "insufferable egocentric bore," for example. The best some can offer is "difficult" or "argumentative." Some say things such as: "He was an impossible person to deal with, but all who could survive his insults thought the world of him."

The other particularly interesting and charming thing about British obituaries is their coded nature. They obviously take seriously the injunction not to speak ill of the dead. So there is an easily crackable code. "He never married" usually means he was a closet gay. "A bon viveur" means he had a drink problem. "He had a small circle of close friends" means he could be difficult, probably with nil social intelligence. "He did not suffer fools gladly" frequently means a bully and gratuitously rude.

There are various stories, both fictional and true, of people reading their own obituaries, visiting their own graves or attending their own funerals. All as a result of error, but all leaving a mark. Who pitches up? What is said? What is left out? Are they "balanced" or singularly eulogistic? Are they disinterested evaluations of a life, or words of comfort approximating the truth to console relatives and supporters?

For some years, the more adventurous business course trainers have required people to write their own obituaries. They are given a model in terms of length and style and told to get on with it. The aim is to be reflective, to evaluate what they have really achieved; what has been their legacy. The questions are "What do you want your life to represent?" "What do you want to be remembered for?" "What have been your (real/only/special) accomplishments?"

The trainers say it's about clarifying your values, about setting a fresh direction and a destiny. Can you sum up your qualities in three words? Do you like them? And, more important, what are you going to do about it if you don't?

It is a sort of task of self-awareness. People who know each other relatively well are encouraged to write their own and their friends' obituaries, and then do a comparison. Even get feedback from others as to how accurate you are in your self-appraisal.

This task can invite false humility. But it is more likely to flush out deluded narcissism and unreconstructed hubris. The minor politicians, civic dignitaries or founders of small businesses who have long been "big fish in a small pool" may be quite mistaken about their talents and contribution. Others may fall victim to the mission/values statement nonsense found in organizations, where there is no relationship, and possibly the opposite, between what they say they value and believe in and how they actually behave.

An exercise like this usually starts with a lot of nervous laughter and chatter. But give people half a day to work on it with no distractions and it can be a very powerful exercise. It works best with "more mature" people, or those who have experienced either a bereavement or ill-health, as they understand the fragility and capriciousness of life.